S0-BFH-430

99
MARI LAJOS
KÁROLY HEMZŐ
HUNGARIAN DISHES
with
33
COLOUR PHOTOGRAPHS

Corvina

Translated by Anna Nilsen
Design by Vera Köböl

On the cover: Mutton stew

Second printing

Printed in Hungary, 1999
Offset Printing House, Budapest

ISBN 963 13 4790 7

FOREWORD

A fresh green patch on the map of Europe embraced by the Alps and the Carpathians, this is Hungary, lying at the crossroads of migration, caravan and campaign routes, a bridge extending between the Eastern and the Western world. The occupying Magyars had the right idea when they got out of the saddle to settle here, because this is a good place to live – but they never suspected that some "transit passengers" would also like the place enough to want to stay for over 150 years, others for a shorter time...

One winner in all this is unquestionably the Hungarian cuisine, which has absorbed and accepted the best flavours and finest traditions of the fiery herdsman and the monk in the monastery garden, of the Turks and the Armenians, the Italians and the Russians, the French and the Jews, the Transylvanians and the neighbouring peoples, of the cuisines of the old Austro-Hungarian empire – tempering and harmonizing them, adjusting them a little to its own image, but preserving them in peace. This most probably explains why – to show a slight lack of modesty and quote Pál Kövi, author of *Erdélyi lakoma* (A Feast from Transylvania) – the Transylvanian (Hungarian) cuisine ranks alongside those of France and China.

But what is Hungarian cooking like? What makes it different from the rest? What are the features which characterise it and it alone? Are there indeed any such features?

I am reminded of our foreign friends and acquaintances who, depending on which part of the world they come from and on the local eating habits, either eloquently praise the flavours and variety of Hungarian foods, or disapprove of them out of concern for their health. But most agree that although it is a little difficult, and might use paprika – sometimes sharp paprika – to excess, all in all, Hungarian cooking is heavenly and unique. (And even those who worry about their health can't resist taking home some paprika, a couple of sticks of salami or sausage, maybe a little goose liver, as a souvenir.)

What makes Hungarian cooking what it is? The ubiquitous smoked bacon? – The Romans already used that in their cooking, and many others after them. Or the sometimes sweet, sometimes sharp paprika? Possibly, though only the improved strain of paprika ripened and dried by the sun on the Alföld plains is a Hungarian "invention"; its cousins are used in abundance in Mediterranean, Arab, Chinese, Far Eastern, Mexican and South American cooking. Maybe the justly world-famous Makó onions with their flavour and thick juice? The quivering firm soured cream and crumbly sweet cow's curd cheese? The tender meats, vibrant vegetables and fragrant fruits? Or the delicious wines which intoxicate and accompany the meals? Possibly; but I think what really makes Hungarian cooking what it is is that whilst keeping the basics, everyone still does things a little differently, according to how their mother or grandmother cooks – that is to say, according to the region they come from. (I have witnessed a spectacular family quarrel over the one authentic way to make stuffed cabbage.) You would think that, in a country so small that barely 500 km (312 miles) now separate its two most distant points, there can't be much variation between the traditions, culture and cuisines of the different regions. But fortunately there is, and each strives to preserve its own, thus adding more colour to the whole.

Hungarians like to do things in style, extending to themselves when they can – and to their guests even more – the courtesy of using good ingredients to prepare food and drink with pleasure and enthusiasm.

Mari Lajos

The recipes are for four people, unless otherwise indicated.

SOUPS

TISZA FISHERMAN'S SOUP (Tiszai halászlé)

500 g (1 lb)	small fish
1	carp and/or other large fish weighing 1–1.2 kg (2–2½ lb)
	salt
1	large onion, finely chopped
1 tbsp	slightly sharp paprika
1	tomato, peeled and chopped
½	cherry paprika (optional)
1	pointed sharp green pepper

Clean and gut the fish and wash them, catch the blood and set it aside, together with the roe or milt, in a cold place. Cut off the head and tail of the carp, and cut the body into strips about 3 cm (1 in) wide – if the strips are narrower, they can easily disintegrate during cooking. Lightly salt the fish, cover it, and leave it for 1–2 hours in a cold place. Put the head and tail of the carp into a saucepan with the small fish. Add the onion and the reserved blood, pour in enough cold water to just cover the fish, and simmer gently for about 1 hour until it is reduced to a pulp. Strain through a fine sieve – don't press! – and pour in about 1 litre (1¾? pints) cold water; bring to the boil. Add the paprika, the tomato, the cherry paprika (if desired), the salted fish slices and the reserved roe or milt, cover the pan and cook over a low heat for 10–15 minutes, until the fish is tender. It's not a good idea to stir the soup – it's better to give the saucepan a gentle shake occasionally.
The finished soup should be served in the saucepan if possible, to avoid the fish breaking up. You can add a garnish of green pepper rings.
Note: Be careful when using cherry paprika. Not everyone likes its burning sharp taste; also, if it is very sharp, the characteristic fish flavour is lost. The remedy for burning hellfire in your mouth as a result of an overdose of sharp paprika is not a drink of water, but a few mouthfuls of bread (the middle, not the crust)!

REVELLER'S FISH SOUP (Korhely halleves)

1	lean carp weighing about 1½ kg (3 lb)
	salt
1	medium onion, peeled and quartered
½	lemon, washed and cut into rings
6–8	fresh tarragon leaves or ½ tsp ground tarragon
8–10	peppercorns
2	bay leaves
½ tsp	noble-sweet paprika
200 ml (7 fl oz)	soured cream
1 teaspon	flour
	lemon juice
1	small bunch parsley

Tisza fisherman's soup

Clean the fish inside and out, wash and fillet it, cut it into 2 cm (1 in) cubes and salt it lightly. Put the bones, head and tail in a saucepan with 2 litres (3½ pints) cold water and bring to the boil. Add the onion, lemon, tarragon, peppercorns, bay leaves and a pinch of salt, and simmer gently over a low heat for 1½ hours.
Put the salted fish with its juices into a saucepan, sprinkle the paprika on top, then strain the hot fish stock over it and return to the boil. Mix the flour and soured cream until smooth, and add to the soup. Return to the boil, then simmer over a low heat for 10–15 minutes, and sharpen to taste with lemon juice.
Transfer the soup to a tureen, scatter chopped parsley on top, and serve immediately.
You could accompany the soup with slices of home-made bread or rolls, rubbed with garlic and toasted.
This soup is an excellent tonic for those suffering from a hangover (and for their stomachs) – but I would also warmly recommend it to non-drunkards!

HUNGARIAN STYLE GULYÁS (GOULASH) SOUP (Magyaros gulyásleves)

	For the pörkölt:
1 tbsp	oil
1	medium onion
1 tsp	noble-sweet paprika
400 g (14 oz)	beef or pork
1	green pepper
1	tomato
	salt
	Also:
200 g (7 oz)	mixture of carrots and parsnips
300 g (11 oz)	potatoes
	caraway seeds

First prepare the *pörkölt*: wash the meat and cut it into 2 cm (1 in) cubes; peel and chop the onion; core the green pepper and cut it into rings; peel the tomato, remove the pips, and cut it into thin strips. Fry the onion in the oil until it is just softened. Remove from the heat and sprinkle the paprika over the onion, add the meat, and fry over a strong heat for a few minutes, stirring constantly. Add the green pepper and the tomato, salt to taste, cover the pan, and braise in its own juices over a moderate heat until almost tender.
Meanwhile, peel and slice the carrots and parsnips, and peel and dice the potatoes. Add them to the meat, and pour in enough cold water for the amount of soup you want to make (about 1.2 litres or

Hungarian style gulyás (goulash) soup

2 pints). Season with a pinch of caraway seeds, and simmer until everything is as soft as butter, adding more salt if necessary.
Serve hot. You could add a garnish of green pepper rings and serve sharp cherry paprika on a separate plate.
Note: 1. in some regions *csipetke* (see Jókai bean soup) are also added to the soup, which makes it almost filling enough to be a meal in itself.
2. Gulyás soup should not be confused with gulyás, the latter being made without vegetables but with double the quantity of potatoes, cut into larger chunks.

CHICKEN RAGOUT SOUP WITH DRIPPED DUMPLINGS (Szárnyasraguleves – csurgatott tésztával)

	giblets from 1 chicken
400 g (14 oz)	mixed vegetables
1	small cauliflower
250 g (9 oz)	peas, shelled
1	medium onion
1	green pepper
1	tomato
2	cloves garlic
8–10	peppercorns
	salt and pepper
1 bunch	parsley, chopped

For the dripped dumplings:

1	egg
3	level tbsp flour
1	pinch salt
50 ml (2 fl oz)	milk

Wash and chop the chicken giblets and put them into a large saucepan. Peel, wash and chop the vegetables as appropriate. Leave the onion, the green pepper and the tomato whole, and put the garlic and the peppercorns into an infuser. Add the vegetables and the infuser to the giblets, pour in 1½ litres (2½ pints) water, season with salt to taste, cover and cook over a moderate heat for 30–35 minutes, until tender. When the soup is ready, remove the infuser, the onion, the green pepper and the tomato, and check the seasoning.
To make the dripped dumplings, combine the egg, flour, salt, and milk, and mix well, then allow the mixture to drip through a narrow funnel into the soup – hence the name (if the mixture is not liquid enough, add 1 or 2 tbsps milk). Scatter the chopped parsley over the soup and serve immediately.
Note: The dripped dumplings should only be boiled briefly in the soup immediately before serving, or else they will "drink" it!

ÚJHÁZY CHICKEN SOUP (Újházy tyúkleves)

Serves 6–8

1	mature chicken weighing 1.8 – 2 kg (3¾ – 4 lb)
800 g (1¾ lb)	soup vegetables (carrots, parsnips, celeriac, kohlrabi)
1	medium onion
2	cloves garlic, peeled
100 g (4 oz)	Savoy cabbage
1	green pepper
1	tomato
10–15	peppercorns
2 pinches	saffron
	salt
100 g (4 oz)	mushrooms
100 g (4 oz)	asparagus, cauliflower or Brussels sprouts
200 g (7 oz)	frozen peas
50 g (2 oz)	noodles
	a few sprigs of parsley

Wash the chicken and put it in a large saucepan. Pour in enough cold water to cover the chicken amply, and bring to the boil without a lid. Meanwhile, peel the soup vegetables and cut them into large chunks. Peel the onion and wash the Savoy cabbage, green pepper and tomato, leaving them whole. Put the garlic, peppercorns and saffron into an infuser and add to the soup with the vegetables and a little salt. Reduce the heat, cover the saucepan, and simmer gently until everything is tender.

Újházy chicken soup

Wipe and slice the mushrooms, wash the asparagus and cut into 5 cm (2 in) spears, and put both into a small saucepan with the peas. Strain 1 or 2 ladlefuls of the soup on top, cover the saucepan, and braise until tender (don't stir, they will break up if you do!); keep warm.
Carefully remove the cooked chicken from the soup and cut it up into smaller pieces, removing the larger bones and the skin. Ladle some hot soup over the pieces and keep warm. Remove the mixed vegetables cooked in the soup, cut into thin slices on a chopping board and add to the vegetables braised separately. Discard the Savoy cabbage, onion, tomato, green pepper, and the contents of the infuser. Skim the fat off the surface of the soup, strain it ladle by ladle, and leave it to settle. Cook the noodles in a separate saucepan in a little of the soup.
Warm a deep soup tureen by rinsing it with hot water. Put the meat, noodles and vegetables in the tureen and ladle the hot soup on top. Chop the parsley finely and scatter it over the soup. Serve immediately.
Just out of interest: this soup, which is almost a meal in itself, was named after Ede Újházy, a popular actor in Budapest at the turn of the century.

SOUR EGG SOUP (Savanyú tojásleves)

30 g (1 oz)	margarine or oil
30 g (1 oz)	flour
1 level tsp	sugar
1	small onion, peeled and grated
1	clove garlic, crushed
½ tsp	noble-sweet paprika
1 litre (1¾ pints)	meat stock
1	bay leaf
	salt and pepper
2 tbsps	wine vinegar
4	eggs
100 ml (4 fl oz)	soured cream
2–3	sprigs of parsley, chopped

Fry the flour in the margarine or oil until golden, add the sugar and carry on frying the mixture, stirring constantly, until it is a dark brown colour. Add the onion and the garlic to the mixture and fry together for 1 minute, then remove the saucepan from the heat, sprinkle the paprika over the roux, immediately pour in 200 ml (7 fl oz) cold water and mix until smooth. Add the stock, wine vinegar and bay leaf, season with salt and pepper to taste, and simmer over a moderate heat for 15 minutes.
One at a time, break the eggs into a small ladle and carefully lower them into the gently simmering soup, taking care not to let them spread. Cook for 3 minutes, just long enough for the whites to set, encasing the yolks. Serve immediately, putting 1 tbsp of soured cream into each plate and ladling the hot soup on top, with one egg per person. Scatter the chopped parsley on top.
Note: This soup is best eaten fresh, while the egg yolks are semi-soft; if they are allowed to stand for a long time in the hot soup or if the soup is reheated, the yolks will become hard and rubbery.

LIVER DUMPLING SOUP (Májgaluskaleves)

2	dry bread rolls
250 ml (8 fl oz)	milk
2 tbsps	butter or margarine
1	small onion
120 g (4 oz)	poultry or calf's liver
1	egg
1	small bunch parsley, chopped
1	clove garlic, crushed
1 tsp	crumbled marjoram
	salt and pepper
1 litre (1¾ pints)	meat stock (can be made with stock cubes)
1	small bunch chives, chopped

Remove the crust from the rolls and soak them in the milk. Chop the onion finely and fry it in the butter until just softened, then leave to cool. Remove the sinews and membranes from the liver and mince it finely; then squeeze the milk thoroughly out of the rolls and mince them too. Add the onion, egg, parsley, garlic and marjoram, and season with salt and pepper to taste. Mix together well, cover, and leave in a cold place for 30 minutes.
Bring 2½ litres (4½ pints) salted water to the boil, then use two teaspoons to cut small dumplings from the mixture and put them into the water. Simmer gently for 7–8 minutes. Meanwhile heat the stock, then use a draining spoon to transfer the dumplings from the water into the hot stock. Scatter the chives over the top and serve hot.
Note: To enrich the soup, cook 100–150 g (4–5 oz) chopped mixed vegetables such as carrots, peas, asparagus in the meat stock before adding the dumplings.

FILLED PASTA POCKETS FOR SOUP

What these filled pasta pockets have in common is that they are all cooked in and served together with strong bone or meat consommés made with a lot of vegetables. Thus they are smaller than the ones eaten "dry", but generally more boldly seasoned.

	For the pasta:
100 g (4 oz)	flour
	salt
2	eggs

Combine the flour, a pinch of salt, one whole egg and the yolk of the other (the white will be needed to brush the edges of the pasta) and knead into a dough. Form a loaf shape and roll it out nice and thin. Put small heaps – about the size of a hazelnut – of the desired filling on one half of the pasta sheet 2–3 cm (1 in) apart. Spread the egg white over the pasta between the heaps of filling, then fold over the other half of the pasta sheet and press down firmly around the filling (to expel the air, otherwise they will burst during cooking). Use a knife, pastry cutter or other implement to cut it up into the desired shapes.

1. Lung pockets (Tüdős táska)

200 g (7 oz)	pig's or calf's lung
1	bay leaf
1 pinch	marjoram
	salt and pepper
30 g (1 oz)	butter or oil
1	small onion
1	egg
30 g (1 oz)	breadcrumbs
1	small bunch parsley

Cook the lung in slightly salted water with the bay leaf and the marjoram until tender. Leave to cool in its own juices, then drain and mince it.
Grate the onion and fry it in the butter until just softened; leave it to cool slightly. Add the lung, the egg, the breadcrumbs and the chopped parsley, season with salt and pepper to taste, and mix together well. Use the mixture to fill the pasta sheet and cut with a pastry cutter into 3 cm (1 in) squares.

2. Brain pockets (Velős derelye)

200 g (7 oz)	pig's or calf's brain
30 g (1 oz)	fat
1	medium onion
100 ml (4 fl oz)	milk
1	dry bread roll
1	egg
1	small bunch parsley, finely chopped
	salt and pepper

Wash the brain, scald it with boiling water, then rinse it with cold water, remove the membranes, and chop it finely.
Chop the onion finely, fry it in the fat until just softened, and leave to cool. Soak the roll in the milk, then squeeze it out thoroughly and add it to the onion together with the brain, the egg and the parsley. Add salt to taste, season generously with pepper, and mix well.
Cut the pasta sheet into 4 cm (1½ in) squares, put a little filling on each square, brush the edges with egg white, and fold diagonally.

3. Tailor's collars (Szabógallér)

200 g (7 oz)	lean pork mince
30 g (1 oz)	fat
1	medium onion
½ tsp	paprika
1	egg
1	small bunch parsley, chopped
	salt and pepper

Chop the onion finely and fry it in the fat until transparent; mix in the paprika, then add the mince and a little salt, cover, and braise the mince in its own juices until tender. Boil away the juices completely, and leave to cool. Add the egg, the chopped parsley, and salt and pepper to taste, and mix together well. Use the mixture to fill the pasta sheet and use a pastry cutter to cut it into small triangles or "tailor's collars" with scalloped edges.

4. Beggar's pockets, or crackling pockets (Koldustáska, or tepertős derelye)

150 g (5 oz)	crackling
1	small onion, finely chopped
	salt and pepper

Mince the crackling, mix in the onion, add salt and pepper to taste, and braise in a small saucepan over a moderate heat for 4–5 minutes. Leave to cool. Use the mixture to fill the pasta sheet, and cut it into 3 cm (1 in) squares, or use a brandy glass to cut crescent shapes.

BEEF SOUP (Marhahúsleves)

1 kg (2 lb)	beef – leg, brisket or loin
500 g (1 lb)	bones, chopped into pieces
500 g (1 lb)	mixed soup vegetables (carrots, parsnips, celeriac, kohlrabi)
1	medium onion
2	cloves garlic
10–15	peppercorns
	trace of cherry paprika
½ level tsp	saffron
1 bunch	parsley
150 g (5 oz)	Savoy cabbage
1	green pepper
1	tomato
	salt
100–150 g	(4–5 oz) pasta for soup

Wash the bones and the meat, cut the meat into 3 or 4 pieces and lay them with the bones in the bottom of a large saucepan. Pour in enough cold water to cover them to a depth of 7 cm (3 in). Bring to the boil (but don't skim off the scum as was always done in the past, because you will lose valuable protein; the scum will settle nicely by itself, and won't make the soup cloudy). Put the peppercorns, garlic, saffron (which will give the soup a beautiful colour), and cherry paprika into an infuser and add to the soup, together with the whole onion, and a little salt. Reduce the

heat and simmer gently, leaving the pan uncovered, for 30 minutes.
Meanwhile, peel the vegetables, cut them into chunks and add them to the soup; then add the Savoy cabbage, green pepper and tomato, leaving them whole (in winter frozen ones are excellent), and the parsley, left in a bunch. Carry on simmering gently, leaving the pan uncovered, until everything is tender.
Cook the pasta, noodles or any other shape, in slightly salted water, then drain it, ladle a little soup over it and keep warm.
Now for the artistry: skim the fat off the surface of the soup, then strain it ladle by ladle through a fine sieve into a warmed soup tureen, tipping the saucepan only very gently in order not to disturb the soup. Place any pieces of vegetable or meat caught in the sieve onto a warmed plate and keep warm. Discard the contents of the infuser, the bones, onion, green pepper, tomato and parsley – they have done their job.
Add the pasta to the hot soup, and serve the vegetables and meat separately – either with the soup or as a second course with various sauces.
Note:
- this soup must not be stirred or it will become cloudy;
- put in a little more water at the start, because it's not a good idea to add water later, it will ruin the taste;
- if you want the soup to be more tasty, put the meat in cold water to cook: the fibres will stay open, allowing the flavours to dissolve into the water;
- if the taste of the meat is more important, put it in boiling water: this will seal the fibres and keep most of the flavour in the meat.

POTATO SOUP WITH CELERY (Krumplileves zellerrel)

600 g (1¼ lb)	potatoes
1	small onion
30 g (1 oz)	fat
30 g (1 oz)	flour
1 tsp	noble-sweet paprika
2 sticks	celery with the leaves
	salt
1 bunch	parsley, chopped

Peel the potatoes and the onion; cut the potatoes into uniform small cubes and chop the onion finely. Fry the flour in the fat until lightly browned, add the onion and fry together for a few minutes, then remove the saucepan from the heat and stir in the paprika. Pour in 200 ml (7 fl oz) cold water, stir until smooth, then add the potatoes and pour in another 1.3 litres (2¼ pints) water. Chop the celery stalk and leaves and add them to the soup, add salt to taste, and simmer over a gentle heat until tender. (Be careful: like all soups made with a roux, it can easily boil over, so put the lid over a wooden spoon laid across the top of the saucepan to vent the soup.) Add the chopped parsley only when the soup is ready, as the valuable vitamin C it contains would be broken down by the heat of cooking.
Flavourful variations:
- enrich the soup with 100 g (4 oz) smoked paprika sausage, sliced thinly and added when the potatoes are almost done;
- enrich it with 200 ml (7 fl oz) soured cream, added after half the cooking time so that it has time to simmer with the soup;
- season it with a little freshly-milled pepper and/or 1 or 2 tbsps tarragon vinegar or lemon juice;
- in summer, add a green pepper cut into thin rings when the soup is almost ready.

LEBBENCS SOUP (Lebbencsleves)

50 g (2 oz)	smoked streaky bacon
200 g (7 oz)	lebbencs pieces or pasta squares
1	small onion
1 tsp	slightly sharp paprika
500 g (1 lb)	potatoes
	salt
1	green pepper
1	tomato
1	small bunch parsley

Cut the bacon into small cubes and fry it until the fat melts, then fry the pasta, broken into fairly large pieces, in the bacon fat. Peel and finely chop the onion and add it to the pasta, and fry together for a few minutes, then sprinkle the paprika on top, and pour in 1½ litres (2¾ pints) water. Peel and dice the potatoes and put them into the soup, add salt to taste, then cover the pan and cook over a moderate heat until everything is tender.
When the soup is ready to serve, wash and core the green pepper, chop the tomato and the parsley, and stir them all into the soup.
This is a quick and nourishing dish – a kind of "poor man's meal" and an ancient shepherds' meal; a few slices of smoked paprika sausage will make it taste even better.
Variation: The soup can be made with *tarhonya* instead of lebbencs.
Lebbencs is a flour and egg dough rolled out thin and cut – or pulled – into large, irregular pieces; *tarhonya* is also an egg pasta, similar in size and shape to rice, and usually served with pörkölt and paprikás dishes.

Beef soup

JÓKAI BEAN SOUP WITH CSIPETKE (Jókai bableves csipetkével)

Serves 4–6

800 g (1¾ lb)	smoked knuckle of ham
250 g (8 oz)	pinto beans
2	bay leaves
2	cloves garlic
8–10	peppercorns
150 g (5 oz)	parsnips
150 g (5 oz)	carrots
100 g (4 oz)	smoked paprika sausage
1 tbsp	oil
30 g (1 oz)	flour
1	medium onion, finely chopped
½ tsp	paprika
200 ml (7 fl oz)	soured cream
	salt
	vinegar or lemon juice
	For the csipetke:
100 g (4 oz)	flour
1	egg
	salt

Place the knuckle and the beans in warm water in separate bowls and soak overnight. Then put the knuckle in a saucepan with enough cold water to cover it and cook until it is half done. Add the rinsed beans, bay leaves, garlic and peppercorns (in an infuser). When the beans are half cooked, add the sliced carrots, parsnips and sausage, and cook until tender.

Meanwhile, prepare the *csipetke:* mix the flour with a pinch of salt, add the egg, and without adding water, knead into a firm dough. Make a small loaf shape, pinch off pieces about the size of a bean, and roll them into balls on a floured board.

When the knuckle is done, remove the bone, cut the meat into small pieces, and return to the soup. Prepare a roux: brown the flour in the oil, add the onion, and fry together for a few minutes. Remove from the heat, sprinkle the paprika over the roux and pour in 300 ml (½ pint) cold water. Stir until smooth, then strain into the soup. Add the soured cream, bring to the boil, add the *csipetke* and cook for 10–12 minutes. Sharpen with vinegar and season with salt to taste; remove the infuser and bay leaves.

Jókai bean soup with csipetke (small dumplings)

You could accompany the soup with more soured cream served in a separate bowl.

Note:

- It is a general rule that the saucepan must be removed from the heat before adding paprika, because it burns very quickly and will give the food a bitter taste.
- The soup can also be thickened with a flour and soured cream mixture instead of a roux.
- *Csipetke* – literally "pinched-off pieces" – are small dumplings, one of many types of dumpling which can be added to soup.

MUSHROOM SOUP WITH VEGETABLES (Zöldséges gombaleves)

1	thin leek
2	medium carrots
1	medium onion
250 g (9 oz)	mushrooms
1 bunch	parsley, chopped
2 tbsps	oil
2	meat stock cubes
	salt and pepper
50 g (2 oz)	rice
200 ml (7 fl oz)	soured cream
1 tbsp	flour
1 tsp	lemon juice

Peel, wash and slice the leek and the carrots; peel and chop the onion. Wipe the mushrooms or rinse them under the tap, and cut the heads into wide strips and the stems into narrow strips. Wash the parsley and chop it finely.

Fry the onion and the leek in the oil until just softened, add the carrots and mushrooms, and fry over a strong heat for a few minutes. Pour in 1 litre (1¾ pints) water, add the stock cubes and season with pepper to taste, then cook over a moderate heat for 10 minutes until half done. Add the rice and cook for a further 10 minutes.

Mix the flour and the soured cream until smooth, add to the soup, and simmer over a low heat for 10 minutes. Finally add the chopped parsley, check the seasoning, and sharpen with the lemon juice.

PALÓC SOUP GUNDEL STYLE, or MIKSZÁTH SOUP (Palócleves Gundel módra or Mikszáth-leves)

300 g (11 oz)	leg or shoulder of mutton (off the bone)
1	large onion
50 g (2 oz)	lard or oil
1 tsp	noble-sweet paprika
1	clove garlic, crushed
1	pinch ground caraway seeds
250 g (9 oz)	green beans
200 g (7 oz)	potatoes
	salt
1	bay leaf
30 g (1 oz)	flour (2 tbsps)
200 ml (7 fl oz)	soured cream
1	small bunch dill

Carefully remove any fat and membranes from the meat, wash it and cut it into small cubes. Scald it, then rinse with cold water and drain thoroughly.

Peel and finely chop the onion and fry it in the fat until just softened. Sprinkle the paprika over it, add the meat, and fry over a strong heat for a few minutes. Reduce the heat, add the garlic and the caraway seeds, cover the pan, and braise the meat in its own juices until tender.

Meanwhile, peel the potatoes, and top and tail the beans, removing the string. Cut the beans into 3 cm (1 in) pieces and the potatoes into small cubes, and cook in slightly salted water in separate saucepans until tender (put the bay leaf in with the beans). Add both, together with their cooking water, to the braised meat (pörkölt), and make the liquid up to 1½ litres (2¾ pints). Mix the flour and the soured cream until smooth, add to the soup, and simmer for a few minutes over a low heat, then check the seasoning. When serving, remove the bay leaf; wash and finely chop the dill and scatter it over the soup.

Note: This heavenly dish was created by János Gundel, the doyen of the Gundel dynasty of restaurateurs, towards the end of the last century, for the writer Kálmán Mikszáth, who was known as the "great Palóc" (the Palóc people being the inhabitants of northern Hungary). Since then it has become a classic, and is also known as Mikszáth soup.

SOUP OF PIG-TRIMMINGS WITH TARRAGON (Tárkonyos malacaprólék-leves)

500 g (1 lb)	pig-trimmings with the skin on (leg, knuckle, head, etc.)
1litre (1¾ pints)	sauerkraut juice
1	large onion
2	cloves garlic
	salt and pepper
100 g (4 oz)	carrots
100 g (4 oz)	parsnips
10–15	dried tarragon leaves
200–300 ml	(about ½ pint) soured cream
30 g (1 oz)	flour
	parsley
	lemon juice

Clean and wash the meat and cut up into pieces. Dilute the sauerkraut juice with 1 litre (1¾ pints) water and bring to the boil. Put in the meat, the whole onion, and the garlic and 10–15 peppercorns

in an infuser, and simmer over a low heat for 30 minutes. Meanwhile, peel and slice the carrots and parsnips, and add them to the soup together with the tarragon, then cover the pan and cook until everything is tender.
Remove the pieces of meat from the soup (removing the bones where necessary) and cut into small pieces; discard the contents of the infuser. Blend the vegetables (including the onion) and the soup in a food processor, and return the meat to the mixture. Mix the flour and soured cream until smooth, stir into the soup, and simmer gently for 5–10 minutes. Add more salt and pepper as necessary, and sharpen with lemon juice or wine vinegar.
When serving, scatter chopped parsley and/or croutons on top.
Note: As with "sour" soups in general, this soup is more tasty if it is prepared the day before, but take care with the salt and lemon juice or vinegar, as these tastes become more emphatic with time.

HUNTER'S SOUP WITH RED WINE (Vörösboros vadászleves)

1	pheasant (or ½ wild duck or ¼ wild goose)
500 g (1 lb)	chopped beef bones
2	cloves
1	large onion
15	peppercorns
4	cloves garlic
350 g (12 oz)	mixed soup vegetables, peeled and chopped
100 g (4 oz)	mushrooms
	salt
30 g (1 oz)	fat
30 g (1 oz)	flour
100 ml (4 fl oz)	red wine
200 ml (7 fl oz)	soured cream
	ground nutmeg
½	lemon
4–5	sprigs parsley

Pluck the fowl, wash it thoroughly, and cut it into 8–12 pieces. Place the pieces on a draining spoon and scald them with boiling water. Wash the beef bones and spread them over the bottom of a large saucepan. Put the meat on top, pour in 2½ litres (4½ pints) cold water, and bring to the boil. Peel the onion, stick the cloves into it, and add it to the soup together with the peppercorns, garlic, soup vegetables, and mushrooms, and a little salt. Simmer gently, uncovered, until the meat comes away easily from the bones (1½–2 hours, depending on the age of the fowl).
Skim the fat off the surface of the soup and strain it. Remove the skin and bones from the meat, and mince it two or three times. Brown the flour in the fat, pour in the soup and stir until smooth. Add the minced meat, wine, soured cream and a pinch of nutmeg, and simmer for 10–15 minutes. Add more salt if necessary, sharpen with a little strained lemon juice, and finally loosely stir in the chopped parsley. The soup must be neither too thick nor emphatically sour. Serve piping hot, with croutons.

COLD MORELLO CHERRY SOUP (Hideg meggyleves)

800 g (1¾ lb)	morello cherries
1	lemon
150 g (5 oz)	sugar or an equivalent amount of sweetener
1 pinch	salt
1	cinnamon stick
6–8	cloves
30 g (1 oz)	flour
200 ml (7 fl oz)	soured cream

Wash, drain and stone the morello cherries. Wash the lemon thoroughly under the hot tap, cut off two strips of peel about 5 cm (2 in) long, then squeeze out and strain the juice. Bring 800 ml (1¼ pints) water to the boil with the sugar and the salt, add the lemon juice, lemon peel, cinnamon, cloves (in an infuser) and the morello cherries, and return to the boil.
Mix the flour and the soured cream until smooth, add it to the boiling soup, and simmer uncovered for 5 minutes over a moderate heat. Remove the saucepan from the heat, cover it to prevent a skin forming, stand it in cold water and leave the soup to cool completely, then refrigerate it for a few hours. To serve the soup,

Cold morello cherry soup

which is best eaten ice cold, remove the cinnamon, the lemon peel and the infuser, and ladle the soup into soup plates or small bowls. You could add a decoration of whipped cream rosettes and chopped almonds.
Note: The soup can be made with any full flavoured fruit, including preserves (use the preserving liquid as well, adjusting the quantities of water, sugar and lemon). Berries with a lot of pips (e.g. currants, goosberrries, raspberries, blackberries) should be pressed through a sieve before the soup is thickened, as the soup will be much more appetising without the pips or peel.

BADACSONY MELON SOUP (Badacsonyi dinnyeleves)

250 g (9 oz)	ripe apricots
4 tbsps	lemon juice
1	honeydew melon weighing about 800 g–1 kg (1¾–2 lb)
500 ml (1 pint)	semi-sweet white Muscatel wine
4–5 tbsps	sugar
1 heaped tbsp	arrowroot
	a few mint leaves
100 ml (4 fl oz)	whipped cream

Wash, halve and stone the apricots, then chop them up and immediately sprinkle them with the lemon juice to prevent them going brown. Wash and dry the melon, cut it in half and remove the pips. Use a melon scoop to make 15–20 balls from the flesh, and set aside for the decoration. Scoop out the remaining flesh with a spoon and add it to the apricots, together with the wine and the sugar. Cover the pan and simmer over a gentle heat for 15 minutes, then purée the fruit in a food processor.
Mix the arrowroot with 2 tbsps of cold water until smooth, add to the soup and heat it just to "boiling point. Leave it to cool completely, then cover and refrigerate for 3–4 hours.
To serve, ladle the soup into attractive plates or deep glass bowls, distribute the melon balls equally among them, and decorate with the mint leaves. You could accompany the soup with whipped cream flavoured with vanilla sugar, served in a separate bowl.

STARTERS AND SALADS

HUNGARIAN STYLE FRIED GOOSE LIVER (Magyaros sült libamáj)

Serves 8

750 g (1½ lb)	goose liver
700–800 ml	(about 1¼ pints) milk
1½ kg (3 lb)	goose fat with the skin on
1	medium onion, peeled and quartered
½ tsp	paprika

Hungarian style fried goose liver

Soak the goose liver for 1 hour in enough cold milk to cover it, then drain it and carefully pat it dry (otherwise it will spit when you fry it). Carefully pluck the goose fat, clean, wash and dice it. Braise it with 300–400 ml cold water and the onion, then fry it until the fat melts, strain it, and press the fat out of the crackling. Put the the liver into a small saucepan just big enough to contain it, carefully ladle the hot fat over it (if possible, cover it completely, in order to avoid having to turn it while frying, as it might break up), and fry gently for 25–30 minutes until browned and tender.
To serve hot: lift the liver out of the fat and place it on a rack to drain, then slice it thinly. Dust the surface with a little salt and paprika, if desired. Serve the crackling, cooled to room temperature, in a separate bowl. You could accompany it with chips, or rice – on its own or mixed with peas.
This dish is more frequently eaten cold: place the liver in a deep glass or china bowl, strain the goose fat over it, cover it, and chill it thoroughly. To serve, scrape off the fat (serve this in a separate bowl), cut it into 3 mm (1/8 in) thick slices, arrange them on a serving dish and dust them with salt and paprika. Serve with fresh home-made bread or toast. You could accompany it with spring onions, green peppers and tomatoes.
Note: If the liver is completely covered by the fat, it will keep in the refrigerator for 3–4 weeks – provided it lasts that long!

MUSHROOMS IN BREADCRUMBS WITH GOOSE LIVER (Rántott gomba libamájjal)

16	medium field or boletus mushrooms (about 600 g / 1¼ lb)
	salt
2 tbsps	lemon juice
100 g (4 oz)	flour
3–4	eggs, beaten
100 g (4 oz)	breadcrumbs
	oil for frying
	a few lettuce leaves
4	sprigs parsley
	For the stuffing:
40 g (2 oz)	butter or margarine
1	medium onion
400 g (14 oz)	goose liver
	salt and ground white pepper
	crumbled marjoram
2 tbsps	flour
100 ml (4 fl oz)	milk
2	egg yolks
50 ml (2 fl oz)	cognac

Wipe the mushrooms and break off the stems. Cook the heads for 5 minutes in boiling water to which a little salt and lemon juice have been added, then drain them and leave them to dry on a tea towel.
Prepare the stuffing: chop the onion finely and fry it in the butter. Slice the goose liver and chop the mushroom stems and add them to the onion. Season with salt, pepper, and a pinch of marjoram, then cover the pan and braise the mixture over a low heat for about 15 minutes, until tender. Scatter the flour over the liver mixture, gradually pour in the milk, and cook for another 5 minutes. Remove from the heat, press the mixture through a sieve, and stir in the egg yolks one at a time. Leave to cool to room temperature, then add the cognac and beat until creamy.
Turn 8 of the mushroom heads hollow side up, fill them with the cream, and place the other 8 mushroom heads on top, pressing down lightly. Coat each "sandwich" with flour, beaten egg, and finally breadcrumbs, then fry them in plenty of hot oil until browned on both sides. Place them on a paper towel to absorb the oil.
Lay the lettuce leaves on a serving dish and arrange the mushrooms on top, garnish with the parsley, and serve immediately. You could accompany it with tartare sauce, served in a separate bowl.
This is a delicious (and expensive) dish, and is recommended as a starter for special occasions.
Note: A quicker variation is to use goose liver braised in its own fat.

MEAT-FILLED PANCAKES HORTOBÁGY STYLE (Hortobágyi húsos palacsinta)

	For 12 pancakes
400 g (14 oz)	veal, lean pork, or chicken breast fillets
1	green pepper
1	tomato
50 g (2 oz)	smoked streaky bacon
1	large onion, finely chopped
1 tsp	slightly sharp paprika
	salt
400 ml (¾ pint)	soured cream (or single cream)
2	sprigs parsley
	For the pancakes:
150 g (5 oz)	flour
3	eggs
	salt
2 tbsps	oil
400 ml (¾ pint)	milk

Rinse and dice the meat. Core the green pepper and slice it into rings, and peel and quarter the tomato. Cut the bacon into small cubes and fry it, then fry the onion in the bacon fat, with the pan covered, until just softened. Add the meat and seal it over a strong heat, then remove the saucepan from the heat, sprinkle the paprika over the meat, and add the green pepper, the tomato, and salt to taste. Mix well, cover the

Meat-filled pancakes Hortobágy style

pan, and braise the meat in its own juices over a moderate heat for 35–40 minutes, until tender.
Meanwhile, make the pancakes: combine the flour, eggs, salt, milk and oil, and stir until smooth. Heat a medium-sized non-stick frying pan and pour in a ladleful of the mixture, allowing it to spread evenly over the bottom of the pan. Fry the pancake over a strong heat for 1 minute on each side, then slide it onto a flat dish. Continue until all the mixture is used up.
Remove the meat from its juices and chop it finely, or mince it. Mix three quarters of the soured cream into the juice, and simmer for a few minutes. Add enough of it to the meat to obtain a spreadable paste. Spread the mixture onto the pancakes, fold in the edges and roll them up. Place the filled pancakes in a row on an attractive heatproof dish, pour the remaining juice over them, and bake in a preheated oven (200°C / 400°F / gas mark 6) for 10 minutes.
To serve, pour the remaining soured cream over the pancakes and garnish with parsley.
This is a very filling starter, so if it's to be followed by a substantial main course, reckon 1 or at most 2 pancakes per person.

STUFFED ONIONS MAKÓ STYLE (Makói töltött hagyma)

4	large onions
	salt and pepper
2 tbsps	oil
200 g (7 oz)	minced pork (leg or shoulder)
1 tsp	paprika
1	clove garlic, crushed
1	pinch ground caraway seeds
1	egg
100 g (4 oz)	tomatoes
200 g (7 oz)	green peppers
1 tbsp	butter or margarine
200 ml (7 fl oz)	soured cream
2	sprigs parsley

Peel the onions and cut a large slice off the top of each (about a quarter of the onion), then scoop out the inside, leaving 3 or 4 layers. Put them in boiling salted water and parboil for 5 minutes, then place them in cold water to cool, and leave them upturned on a clean tea towel to drain.
Prepare the stuffing: chop the "caps" and the scooped out onion flesh finely, and fry it in the oil until transparent. Add the mince and fry over a strong heat for a few minutes, then scatter the paprika on top, add a little salt and pepper, and the crushed garlic and the caraway seeds. Cover the pan, and braise the meat in its own juices over a moderate heat until tender. Then use a draining spoon to remove the mince mixture from the juices, place it in a deep bowl, and leave it to cool to room temperature. Then stir in the egg, and stuff the onions with the mixture.

Peppers stuffed with curds

While the meat is cooling, peel the tomatoes and cut them into segments, and core the green peppers and cut them into rings. Add both to the meat juices, and braise until they almost disintegrate, then transfer them to a heatproof serving dish. Place the stuffed onions on top, brush with melted butter, cover with foil, and bake in a preheated oven for 25–30 minutes, until tender. Serve as a starter, with soured cream poured over the top and garnished with parsley leaves.

PEPPERS STUFFED WITH CURDS (Körözöttel töltött paprika)

250 g (8 oz)	ewe's curds
125 g (4 oz)	butter or margarine
4	fleshy peppers
1	onion
12–15	stems chives
1 tsp	mustard
1 tsp	noble-sweet paprika
1 tsp	paprika purée
½ tsp	ground caraway seeds
4 tbsps	lager
	salt and pepper

Take the curds and the butter out of the refrigerator 1 hour beforehand to allow them to soften. Wash and core the peppers, removing the veins. Peel and grate the onion. Wash the chives, shake off the excess water and chop them finely.

Beat the curds with the butter, onion, mustard, paprika, paprika purée, caraway seeds, lager and a little freshly milled pepper until creamy, then add the chives. Add salt only at the very end, having tasted the mixture first (beware – a lot of the ingredients are themselves salty!).
Stuff the peppers with the mixture, packing it in well, then wrap them in aluminium foil and put them in a cold place for at least 2 hours. To serve, cut the peppers into 1 cm (½ in) thick slices and lay these on lettuce or vine leaves. You could accompany them with fresh home-made bread, toast, or slices of roll fried in garlic butter, and tomatoes or spring onions.
This is an excellent accompaniment for drinks, and ideal for outings and picnics.
Variation: Pile the curd mixture into an attractive bowl, make a pattern on the top with a fork, and garnish with parsley or chives.

GOURMET LETTUCE SALAD (Ínyenc fejes saláta)

2	lettuces
400 ml (¾ pint)	water
2 tbsps	sugar
1 tsp	salt
2 tbsps	wine or cider vinegar
	For the dressing:
2	hard boiled eggs
200 ml (7 fl oz)	soured cream
1 tsp	mustard
	salt and pepper

Remove the outer leaves, and any which are bruised or hardened, from the lettuces, then either separate the leaves, or cut the lettuces into 2–4 pieces, depending on their size. Wash them thoroughly twice, then drain them or spin them dry.
Stir the sugar and salt into the water until dissolved, and add the wine vinegar. Pour the mixture into a deep bowl and toss the lettuce in it, then drain the lettuce and put it onto 4 small plates.
Peel the boiled eggs, finely grate the whites and one of the yolks, then add the soured cream, mustard, and salt and freshly-milled pepper to taste. Pour the mixture over the lettuce portions. Grate the remaining egg yolk on top, and serve immediately.

CUCUMBER SALAD WITH SOURED CREAM AND GARLIC (Tejfölös-fokhagymás uborkasaláta)

500 g (1 lb)	cucumbers
1	medium onion
	salt and pepper
200 ml (7 fl oz)	soured cream
2	cloves garlic, crushed
1 bunch	dill, finely chopped
½ tsp	paprika

Wash the cucumbers thoroughly and peel them with a potato peeler (if the skin isn't too thick, leave them unpeeled and wipe them dry), then slice them wafer-thin. Peel the onion, slice it thinly, and add it to the cucumber. Salt lightly, mix together, cover the bowl, and leave to stand for 1 hour.
Mix together the soured cream, garlic, dill and a little freshly-milled pepper. Pour the mixture over the cucumber, mix well, cover the bowl, and refrigerate. When serving, sprinkle paprika over the salad.
Variations:
- enrich the salad by adding 1 finely diced red pepper;
- instead of the soured cream dressing, use a mixture of 4 tbsps wine vinegar, 100 ml (4 fl oz) water, a little pepper, salt to taste, and ½ tsp caster sugar;
- you could add 1–2 tbsps oil to the salad, and sharpen it with lemon juice instead of wine vinegar.

PORK IN ASPIC (Sertéskocsonya)

Serves 8

1 kg (2 lb)	pig trimmings with the skin on (knuckle, trotter, tail, head, ear, bacon rind)
400 g (14 oz)	lean pork or pork tongue
200 g (7 oz)	smoked pork
1	large onion
8–10	cloves garlic
800 g (1¾ lb)	parsnips
½	cherry paprika
20–25	peppercorns
	salt
	paprika

Clean the trimmings carefully, singing off any hairs, and wash them twice, together with the meat. Cut the trimmings and the meat into smaller pieces and put them into a 6–8 litre (10–14 pint) saucepan. Wash the onion but don't peel it (this will give the aspic its lovely colour), and leave it whole. Peel the garlic and the parsnips, put the cherry paprika and the peppercorns into an infuser, and add them all to the meat. Pour in enough water to cover it well, as liquid which evaporates during cooking can't be replaced by adding more water later. Bring to the boil, skim off the scum with a draining spoon, add a little salt, then half cover the pan and simmer gently for 2–2½ hours. Carefully skim the fat off the surface of the liquid, strain it through a fine strainer, add more salt if necessary, and leave it to settle. Remove the parsinps, the onion, the contents of the infuser, and the larger bones. Distribute the trimmings, the meat and the smoked meat equally into 8 bowls or soup plates and ladle on enough liquid to almost cover it. Cover the

bowls and leave them in a cold place (3–4 hours will be needed for the liquid to set completely).
To serve, decorate the rims of the plates with lemon or onion rings, parsley leaves, or chives, and sprinkle paprika over the aspic, if desired. You could sprinkle on a few drops of wine vinegar or lemon juice, and serve with pickles, horseradish in vinegar, or sliced pickled onions. The best accompaniment is fresh crusty bread.

Suggestions:

- If you prefer it completely fat-free, it is worth cooking it the night before and leaving it in a cold place overnight, then the next day you can remove all the set fat from the surface. Warm it up over a moderate heat, then continue as above.
- If time and patience permit, the serving method can be a little more elaborate: "line" a ring mould or cake tin with a little aspic and leave it in a cold place to set, then decorate all over with braised vegetables (e.g. beetroot, carrots, peas), gherkins, and slices of hard-boiled egg, and finally add the meat and remaining aspic.

Note: Like consommé, meat in aspic shouldn't be kept longer than 3–4 days, even in a cold place, as it will go off.

FISH

FRIED PIKE-PERCH CRESCENTS (Kunkori süllősült)

	Serves 6
3	pike-perches each weighing 600–700 g (1¼ – 1½ lb)
	salt
100 g (4 oz)	flour
1 tsp	paprika
	oil for frying
3	slices of bread 2–3 cm (1–1¼ in) thick
	For the garnish:
1	lettuce
6	peas

Fried pike-perch crescents

Clean and wash the fish, and make cuts into the flesh at right angles to the spine, cutting through the ribs, then salt and leave for 1 hour. Combine the flour and paprika and coat the fish with the mixture, then heat up a 5–7 cm (2½–3 in) depth of oil in a saucepan just big enough to hold the fish curved into a semicircle. If you want to make sure that the fish will be curved, or if you haven't got a saucepan the right size (in which case use a large, deep baking tray, still on the hob), then use a large needle and strong thin string to fasten the upper lip and tail of the fish together.

Place each fish in turn into the hot oil and fry it, without covering the pan, for 5–8 minutes on ech side, turning it carefully with two fish slices. Place the fish onto paper towels to absorb the oil, and keep warm. Cut out the middle of the bread slices, leaving 1 cm (½ in) inside the crust (these will be "dry docks" for the fish to prevent them falling over on the serving dish), then fry them in the oil until browned.

Wash and drain the lettuce leaves and use them to line a large serving dish. Place the fried bread crusts onto the lettuce leaves, sit the fish on top, and put a pea into each eye socket.

Serve immediately, accompanied by potatoes boiled in salted water then and tossed in parsley butter or fried, with lemon slices and tartare sauce. This dish must be eaten fresh!

CATFISH AND BACON ROLLS IN GARLIC AND WINE SAUCE (Szalonnás göngyölt harcsa fokhagymás bormártásban)

1.2 kg (2½ lb)	catfish fillets (8 fillets)
	salt and pepper
400 g (14 oz)	tomatoes
8	thin rashers smoked bacon
3–4 tbsps	flour
80 g (3 oz)	butter or margarine
200 ml (7 fl oz)	dry white wine
4	cloves garlic
2	anchovy rings in oil
1	large bunch parsley

Wash the fillets, salt them lightly, and leave them to stand for 30 minutes. Scald and peel the tomatoes, discard the pips, and chop them. Wipe the fillets, lay a rasher of bacon on each, roll them up and secure them with a toothpick, then coat them with the flour. Heat the fat in a deep pan and lightly fry the fish rolls all over. Add half of the wine, and leave to reduce a little. Then put in the tomatoes, season with salt and pepper to taste, cover the pan, and braise the fish over a low heat for 15–20 minutes, until tender. Don't stir, just give the pan a gentle shake occasionally.

Meanwhile, *prepare the sauce:* crush the garlic, drain and crumble the anchovy rings, and chop the parsley finely. Add the rest of the wine, and sprinkle with a little freshly milled pepper. Stir well, pour over the braised fish, and simmer for a few minutes.

Arrange the fish rolls on a warmed serving dish, cover with the sauce, and serve immediately. You could add a garnish of a few slices of tomato or parsley leaves. This dish is best served with a neutral accompaniment of rice or potatoes, which will allow the very emphatic garlic taste to predominate.

DOROZSMA MILLER'S CARP (Dorozsmai molnárponty)

4	large carp fillets (800 g / 1¾ lb)
	salt and pepper
100 g (4 oz)	smoked streaky bacon
1	large onion
3	green peppers
3	tomatoes
200 g (7 oz)	mushrooms
1 tsp	paprika
400 ml (¾ pint)	soured cream
250 g (8 oz)	pasta
4–5 tbsps	breadcrumbs
	oil for frying
	For the garnish:
1	tomato
1	pointed green pepper
1 or 2	sprigs parsley

Wash and drain the carp fillets, salt them, and leave them to stand for 30 minutes. Meanwhile cut the bacon into small cubes and fry it until the fat melts. Peel and slice the onion and fry the rings in the bacon fat until just softened. Wash the vegetables; core the green peppers and cut them into rings; peel the tomatoes and cut them into segments; slice the mushrooms thinly.

Remove the pan from the heat, scatter the paprika over the onions, add the tomatoes, green peppers and mushrooms, and season with salt and pepper to taste. Return to the heat, cover the pan, and cook for 15 minutes until almost tender, then stir in half of the soured cream. Cook the pasta in slightly salted water and drain it. Loosely stir in half of the vegetable mixture, and place it in a heatproof serving dish.

Heat the oil, coat the fish fillets with the breadcrumbs, and fry them until browned on both sides, then arrange them on top of the pasta. Heap the remaining vegetable mixture around the fillets, spread the rest of the soured cream over them, and bake in a hot oven (200°C / 400°F / gas mark 6) for about 30 minutes, until browned. Garnish with slices of tomato and green pepper, and parsley. Serve hot.

Variation: Omit the tomatoes and green peppers and use 500 g (1 lb) mushrooms for the vegetable mixture; crush 2 cloves of garlic, fry in 1 tbsp of margarine or oil until just softened, and stir into the pasta.

Dorozsma miller's carp

TROUT STUFFED WITH CHICKEN LIVER (Csirkemájas töltött pisztráng)

4	trout (about 400 g / 14 oz each)
	salt and pepper
200 g (7 oz)	chicken livers
50 g (2 oz)	raw smoked ham
4 tbsps	butter or margarine
2 tbsps	brandy
	crumbled marjoram
1	medium onion
1 bunch	parsley
1	medium carrot
1 tbsp	breadcrumbs
200 ml	dry white wine

Clean and wash the fish, wipe them dry and rub them with salt and pepper. Wash the chicken liver, remove the membranes, and cut it into small cubes, together with the ham. Beat 2 tbsps of butter and the brandy until light and fluffy, work it loosely into the liver and ham mixture, add 2–3 pinches of crumbled marjoram, then stuff the fish with the mixture and pin the cavities closed.
Peel the vegetables, chop the onion and the parsely finely and cut the carrot into very small pieces. Heat 1 tbsp of the butter, add the vegetables and the breadcrumbs, and fry them over a strong heat for a few minutes, then stir in the wine. Grease an oblong heatproof dish thickly with the remaining butter, lay the stuffed trout in it and cover them with the vegetable and breadcrumb sauce. Cover with foil and bake in a preheated medium oven (180°C / 350°F / gas mark 4) for 25–30 minutes, then remove the foil and continue baking for about 20 minutes, until browned. Serve immediately, accompanied by potatoes boiled in salted water and then tossed in parsley butter or mashed, or rice, or steamed vegetables.

PIKE IN HORSERADISH SAUCE (Csuka tormamártásban)

Serves 6

1	pike (1.2–1.5 kg / 2½–3 lb) or other lean fish
200 g (7 oz)	mixed soup vegetables, peeled and chopped
1	medium onion, peeled and sliced
1	bay leaf
8–10	peppercorns
	salt
1 tbsp	wine vinegar or lemon juice
	For the sauce:
150 g (5 oz)	horseradish
50 g (2 oz)	butter
30 g (1 oz)	flour
	salt
½ tsp	sugar
400 ml (¾ pint)	soured cream
	strained juice of 1 lemon
	parsley

Clean the fish inside and out, and salt it lightly. Pour 1½ litres (2½ pints) water into a fish kettle or deep baking tray, add the vegetables, onion, bay leaf, peppercorns, and a little salt, and cook until almost tender. Sharpen with the wine vinegar or lemon juice, add the fish, and cook for 10 minutes. Keep it warm in its own juices.
For the sauce, peel and grate the horseradish, and scald and drain half of it. Brown the flour in the butter, add 400 ml (¾ pint) of strained fish juice and stir until smooth, then add the scalded and the raw horseradish and the soured cream, and bring to the boil, stirring constantly. Flavour with the lemon juice, the sugar, and salt.
Slide the fish onto a warmed oblong serving dish, cover with the sauce, sprinkle with chopped parsley, and serve immediately.
The best accompaniment is potatoes boiled in salted water and tossed in parsley butter.

BALATON PIKE-PERCH IN CREAMY MUSHROOM SAUCE (Balatoni fogas tejszínes gombamártásban)

1	pike-perch (1.2–1.4 kg / 2½–3 lb)
	salt and pepper
80 g (3 oz)	butter
1	medium onion
1	large bunch parsley
1	sprig (10 cm / 4 in) fresh rosemary
200 ml (7 fl oz)	dry white wine (e.g. riesling)
400 g (14 oz)	mushrooms
2 tbsps	flour
200–300 ml	(about ½ pint) meat stock (made with a stock cube)
200 ml (7 fl oz)	cream

Clean, skin and fillet the fish, and cut it into slices 10–15 cm (4–6 in) wide. Sprinkle it with salt and pepper and leave to stand for 30 minutes. Finely chop the onion, parsley and rosemary, and fry them a little (about 2 minutes) in half of the butter in a large frying pan. Add the fish slices, pour in the wine, cover the pan, and braise over a moderate heat for 6–8 minutes, until tender.
Meanwhile, *prepare the sauce:* wipe the mushrooms, cut them into thin slices or small cubes, and fry them in the rest of the butter. Sprinkle on the flour and gradually pour in the stock, then add the cream, and salt and pepper to taste, and simmer for a few minutes.
Arrange the fish slices on a warmed serving dish and keep warm. Strain the juices out of the pan onto the sauce, return to the boil briefly, then cover the fish

slices with the sauce, and serve immediately, garnished with parsley leaves.
The best accompaniment is boiled potatoes tossed in parsley butter.

ONE-COURSE MEALS

HUNGARIAN STYLE POTATO BAKE (Magyaros rakott krumpli)

1 kg (2 lb)	potatoes
6	eggs
	salt
100 g (4 oz)	smoked paprika sausage
500 ml (1 pint)	soured cream
2	egg yolks
20 g (1 oz)	butter
100 g (4 oz)	smoked streaky bacon

Cook the potatoes in their skins, peel them while still warm, and leave them to cool. Meanwhile, hard boil the eggs in heavily salted water, cool them with cold water, then peel and slice or quarter them; and slice the sausage. Stir the egg yolks into the soured cream with a little salt.
Grease an ovenproof dish with the butter. Slice the potatoes, and lay half the slices in the bottom of the dish. Distribute the egg and sausage slices over the potato, sprinkle with a little salt, and spread half the soured cream mixture on top. Lay the remaining potato slices over the filling so that they overlap slightly, sprinkle with salt, and spread the remaining soured cream mixture evenly on top. Finally, slice the bacon thinly, cut slits in it perpendicular to the rind, and lay the slices on the soured cream topping.
Bake in a preheated hot oven (220°C / 425°F / gas mark 6) for 35–40 minutes, until the soured cream and the bacon are golden brown. Serve with a seasonal mixed salad, or with pickles.

PAPRIKA POTATOES (Paprikás krumpli)

100 g (4 oz)	smoked bacon
1	large onion
1 kg (2 lb)	cooking potatoes
1	green pepper
1	tomato
100 g (4 oz)	smoked paprika sausage
½ tsp	ground caraway seeds
1 tsp	paprika
	salt

Cut the bacon into thin strips or small cubes and fry it. Peel and chop the onion, add it to the bacon, cover the pan, and fry it until just softened. Meanwhile, peel the potatoes and cut them into chunks; core the green pepper and cut it into rings; peel the tomato and cut it into segments.
Wash and slice the sausage, add it to the onion, together with the caraway seeds, and fry together for a few minutes. Remove the saucepan from the heat, add the paprika and the potatoes, and pour on enough water to just cover them. Add the green pepper and tomato, and salt to taste, cover the pan, and cook over a moderate heat until tender.
This dish is generally enriched by cooking frankfurters or other mildly spicy sausages with the potatoes. Serve with pickles or a seasonal salad. Potato-loving guests from abroad rave about this dish!
Note: Make sure that there's enough liquid, because it's best when everyone can mash the potatoes into the juices on their plates.
Variations: some people prefer this dish without caraway seeds; others add 1 or 2 cloves of garlic.

LECSÓ

100g (4 oz)	smoked streaky bacon
2 tbsps	oil
2	large onions
500g (1lb)	tomatoes
1kg (2lb)	green peppers
1 tsp	slightly sharp paprika
	salt

Cube the bacon and fry it in the oil until the fat melts. Chop the onion finely and fry in the bacon fat until just softened. Meanwhile, scald the tomatoes, peel them, and cut them into segments; core the green peppers and cut them into rings. Remove the saucepan from the heat, scatter the paprika over the braised onions, and add the tomatoes. Return to the heat, and allow to boil for a few minutes uncovered, then add the green peppers, and salt to taste, cover the pan, and braise over a moderate heat until tender. Serve with potatoes boiled in salted water and tossed in parsley butter, or steamed rice.
Variation: Enrich with slices of paprika sausage (100 g / 4 oz), or frankfurters cooked in the lecsó – allow 2 per person.
Note: *Lecsó* is the main component of many Hungarian dishes. Its characteristic taste is given by excellent onions, typical Hungarian green peppers (which are actually yellow), and fine, slightly sharp Hungarian paprika.

STUFFED MARROW WITH DILL SAUCE (Töltött tök kapormártással)

2	small tender marrows (1.2 kg – 2½ lb)
	salt and pepper
2 tbsps	vinegar
2 tbsps	oil
1	medium onion

Lecsó

80 g (3 oz)	rice
400 g (14 oz)	minced pork
1	clove garlic, crushed
1	egg
100 ml (4 fl oz)	meat stock (can be made with a stock cube)
30 g (1 oz)	butter or margarine
1	large bunch dill
	grated rind and juice of 1 lemon
40 g (2 oz)	flour
400 ml (¾ pint)	soured cream or single cream

Peel the marrows and cut them in half crosswise. Scoop out the middle, then put the halves in enough water to cover them, add a little salt and vinegar, and parboil them for 10 minutes. Remove them from the juices and drain them.

Prepare the stuffing: chop the onion finely and fry it in the oil until just softened; cook the rice in slightly salted water for 10 minutes, then drain it and leave it to cool. Combine the mince, rice, onion, garlic, egg, and salt and pepper to taste, work together thoroughly, then stuff the mixture into the cavities of the marrow halves. Place the marrows in a heatproof dish, add the stock, cover, and cook in a preheated medium oven (180°C / 350°F / gas mark 4) for 35 minutes; keep warm, and strain the juices.

For the sauce, chop the dill finely and fry it lightly in the butter. Add the marrow juices (add stock or water to make up to 100 ml / 4 fl oz if necessary) and the lemon rind and juice, and bring to the boil. Mix the flour and soured cream to a smooth paste and add it to the boiling juice, then simmer over a gentle heat for 5 minutes, stirring frequently – don't cover the pan, or it will boil over! Cut the marrow halves into 3 cm / 1 in thick slices, pour the sauce on top, and serve hot.

Variation: Use courgettes instead of marrows.

STUFFED SPRING KOHLRABI (Tavaszi töltött karalábé)

8	tender kohlrabis (with leaves)
400 g (14 oz)	minced pork)
1	egg
1	large bunch parsley, finely chopped
	salt and pepper
80 g (3 oz)	cooked rice
500 ml (1 pint)	meat stock made with stock cubes
30 g (1 oz)	butter

Stuffed marrow with dill sauce

40 g (1½ oz)	flour
400 ml (¾ pint)	soured cream (or half as much single cream)

This is really a dish to make in spring, when the kohlrabis are still tender. Peel the kohlrabis and scoop out a hollow from the root end of each. Set aside a few of the largest leaves to wrap around any excess stuffing, then wash the tender inner leaves and cut them into thin strips.
Work together the mince with the egg and 1 tsp of the parsley, add salt to taste, and a generous sprinkling of pepper, and finally add the rice. Loosely fill the hollows in the kohlrabis (and the leaves).
Spread the scooped out kolhrabi bits over the bottom of a large saucepan and place the stuffed kohlrabis and leaf parcels on top. Scatter the leaf strips around the kohlrabis and parcels, pour on the stock, cover the pan, and cook over a low heat until tender. When the kohlrabis are tender, remove them from the liquid with a draining spoon (be careful with the leaf parcels, as they fall apart easily!), and keep them warm.
Lightly brown the flour in the butter, add 200 ml (7 fl oz) cold water and mix until smooth. Strain the mixture into the cooking liquid, then add the soured cream or cream, and boil for 10 minutes. Replace the kohlrabi and leaf parcels in the thickened liquid, heat through, and then gently stir in the remaining parsley. You could accompany the kohlrabis with more soured cream served in a separate bowl.

HUNGARIAN STYLE STUFFED PEPPERS WITH TOMATO SAUCE (Magyaros paradicsomos töltött paprika)

8	medium peppers, not too fleshy
1	small onion
2	tbsps oil
400g (14 oz)	minced pork
80 g (3 oz)	cooked rice
1	egg
1	clove garlic, crushed
½ tsp	noble-sweet paprika
	salt and pepper
1 litre (1¾ pints)	tomato juice or 100 g (4 oz) tomato purée mixed with 1 litre (1¾ pints) cold water
1	stick celery
30 g (1 oz)	flour
1 tsp	caster sugar

Wash the peppers and core them, removing the veins and pips. Peel and chop the onion, fry it in 1 tsp of the oil until just softened, and leave it to cool. Then add the onion to the mince, together with the rice, egg, garlic, paprika, and salt and pepper to taste. Work together thoroughly, then stuff the peppers – not too tightly – with the mixture.
Bring the tomato juice (or diluted purée) to the boil with a little salt and the celery, place the stuffed peppers into the liquid, cover the pan, and cook over a low heat for about 30 minutes until they are tender. Meanwhile, lightly brown the flour in the remaining oil, remove from the heat, add 200 ml (7 fl oz) cold water, and mix until smooth. Remove the cooked peppers with a draining spoon, strain the roux into the tomato juice, and boil for 10 minutes. Discard the celery. Replace the peppers in the sauce, and simmer gently for a further 5 minutes. Add more salt to taste, and sweeten with the caster sugar. Serve with potatoes cooked in salted water and tossed in parsley butter.
Note: If there is stuffing left over, for instance because the peppers are too small to take it all, shape the remainder into small balls and cook these together with the peppers in the tomato juice.

STUFFED CABBAGE (Töltött káposzta)

Serves 4–6

300 g (11 oz)	smoked pork (knuckle, shoulder, leg, spare ribs)
1 kg (2 lb)	sour cabbage (sauerkraut)
8	cabbage leaves (pickled or fresh)
50 g (2 oz)	smoked streaky bacon
1	medium onion
400 g (14 oz)	minced pork (ham or shoulder)
1	egg
80 g (3 oz)	cooked rice
1	clove garlic, crushed
2 tsps	paprika
	salt, pepper
100 g (4 oz)	spicy frankfurter-type sausage (e.g. Debreceni), sliced
1	bay leaf
½	cherry paprika
2 tbsps	oil or fat
30 g (1 oz)	flour
1 tsp	paprika
1	thick rasher smoked bacon
200–300 ml	(about ½ pint) soured cream
	parsley

Place the smoked meat in cold water, bring to the boil and cook until tender; then remove the meat from the stock and set aside. Give the sour cabbage a little rinse and put half of it in the meat stock. Unfold the cabbage leaves (if using fresh cabbage leaves, scald them and leave them to drain), and gently beat the thick central veins to flatten them.
Dice the bacon and fry it until the fat melts. Chop the onion finely, add it to the bacon fat and fry until just softened, then leave to cool. Stir it into the mince, together with the rice, garlic, egg, paprika, salt, and pepper, then divide the mixture evenly between the

Stuffed cabbage

cabbage leaves. Wrap the leaves loosely around the mince mixture and place the parcels on top of the sour cabbage. Cover them with the remaining sour cabbage, add the slices of sausage and the bay leaf (and a small piece of cherry paprika, if desired), cover the pan, and braise over a moderate heat until tender. It's better not to stir – just give the saucepan a shake occaionally. Carefully lift the parcels out of the sour cabbage. Brown the flour in the oil or fat, remove from the heat, and stir in the paprika. Pour in 100 ml (4 fl oz) cold water, stir until smooth, add this roux to the sour cabbage, and bring to the boil. Finally, cut the smoked meat into small pieces, and place it, together with the parcels, into the sour cabbage, check the seasoning, and heat through. Cut slits into the thick rasher of smoked bacon, and fry it. To serve, spoon the sour cabbage into a warmed bowl, place the parcels on top and the fried bacon in the middle, pour the soured cream over the top and garnish with the parsley.

Variation: Cut slits into a spicy sausage, fry it and place this on top instead of the bacon.

Note: This dish can be prepared days before it is needed (it freezes very well), but be careful with the salt, as this dish gets more salty with time. As it burns easily during heating, it is best to heat it covered, over a moderate heat, or in the oven, or in the microwave a little at a time. Don't stir, just shake the saucepan occasionally!

SZÉKELYGULYÁS

500 g (1 lb)	pork shoulder
4 tbsps	oil or lard
1	large onion
1 tsp	paprika
1	green pepper, cored and cut into rings
1	tomato, peeled and chopped
1	clove garlic, crushed
1	pinch caraway seeds
	salt and pepper
800 g (1¾ lb)	sour cabbage
1	bay leaf
400 ml (¾ pint)	soured cream
30 g (1 oz)	flour
1	pointed sharp green pepper

First make a *pörkölt:* wash and dice the meat; chop the onion finely and fry it in the oil or fat until softened, then add the meat and fry over a strong heat until it whitens. Scatter the paprika and caraway seeds over the meat, add the garlic, green pepper rings, tomatoes, and a little salt, cover the pan, and braise the meat in its own juices for about 40 minutes, until tender.

If the cabbage is too salty or sour, rinse it under the cold tap, then braise it with a little water and the bay leaf until tender. If it produces too much liquid, drain it.

Stir the flour into the soured cream, add the mixture to the *pörkölt*, bring to the boil, then stir the *pörkölt* into the cabbage, and simmer for 10 minutes. Discard the bay leaf, and check the seasoning. Transfer to a deep bowl, garnish with slices of green pepper, and serve hot. Accompany with fresh home-made bread and more soured cream in a separate bowl.

Note: The meat and the cabbage ought really to be braised together, but in my experience they often don't take the same amount of time to cook, and as a result one or other of them is overcooked.

This dish is not named after the Székelys (Hungarian inhabitants of Transylvania), but after one particular gentleman named Székely, who ran a homely restaurant from the 1840s onwards in Budapest. Because it was cheap, the young people of the Reform Era ate there regularly. But late one evening all that was left in the kitchen was some *pörkölt* and some braised cabbage, and the young people were very hungry... Apparently the dish was added to the menu as a particular favourite of Sándor Petőfi, one of Hungary's greatest poets.

POTATOES STUFFED WITH EWE'S CURDS (Juhtúrós töltött burgonya)

8	potatoes, 100 g (4 oz) each
	salt and pepper
1	large bunch dill
300 g (11 oz)	ewe's curds
50 g (2 oz)	butter or margarine
1	small onion
300 g (11 oz)	mushrooms, wiped and diced
1	small bunch parsley, chopped
40 g (2 oz)	flour
200 ml (7 fl oz)	bone stock or meat stock made with a stock cube
200 ml (7 fl oz)	single cream

Wash the potatoes and cook them unpeeled in salted water; peel them while still hot and leave them to cool. Set aside a few stalks of dill for the garnish, and chop the remainder finely. Add it to the sheep's curds and stir until creamy. Cut the potatoes in half lengthwise, scoop out the middle of each half, and fill the hollows with the mixture.

Place the potatoes into a baking dish greased with some of the butter, and spread the scooped out potato bits around them.

Prepare the mushroom sauce: fry the onions in the remaining butter until just softened. Add the mushrooms, the parsley, and salt and pepper to taste, and fry for 5 minutes. Scatter the flour over the mixture, gradually pour on the stock, and stir until smooth; then add the cream and boil for 4–5 minutes.

Bake the potatoes in a preheated moderate oven (180°C / 350°F / gas mark 4) until heated through. Serve in the baking dish, garnished with the remaining dill. Serve the sauce in a separate bowl.

BÁCSKA HASH
(Bácskai rizses hús)

500 g (1 lb)	pork shoulder
6 tbsps	oil (or lard)
1	large onion
1 tsp	paprika
300 g (11 oz)	green peppers, washed, cored, and sliced
150 g (5 oz)	tomatoes, peeled and chopped
200 g (7 oz)	long grain rice
	salt and pepper
4–5	stems parsley, chopped

Make a *pörkölt* (see p. 28) with the meat, 4 tbsps of the oil, the onion and the paprika. When the meat is almost tender, add the green peppers and tomatoes, reserving a little of each for the garnish.
Heat the remaining 2 tbsps of oil and fry the rice in it for 2–3 minutes, then add it to the meat. Pour on 400 ml (¾ pint) hot water, add a little salt, stir, and bring to the boil. Transfer to a heatproof serving dish, cover, and bake in a preheated hot oven (200°C / 400°F / gas mark 6) for 20 minutes until the rice is softened. Stir only once, halfway through the baking time.
Garnish with the reserved green pepper and tomato slices and the parsley, and serve immediately.

POULTRY AND LAMB

PAPRIKA CHICKEN WITH DUMPLINGS
(Paprikás csirke galuskával)

2	small chickens, or 1 large one (1.2–1.3 kg)
2 tbsps	oil or fat
1	large onion
1 tsp	slightly sharp paprika
	salt
1	green pepper
1	tomato
400–500 ml	(about 1 pint) soured cream
	For the dumplings:
500 g (1 lb)	flour
2	eggs
½ level tsp	salt
300–400 ml	(about ¾ pint) milk
50 g (4 oz)	butter

Wash and joint the chicken. Chop the onion finely and fry it in the oil or fat over a moderate heat, with the pan covered, until tender. Then remove the pan from the heat, stir in the paprika, pour on 100 ml (4 fl oz) water, add salt, and simmer for a few minutes. Add chicken pieces, the green pepper and the tomato, cover the pan, and braise over a low heat until tender. If too much liquid should evaporate, replace it with very little water, because it's best if the chicken cooks in its own juices.
Remove the green pepper and the tomato, boil to reduce the liquid, then add the soured cream: don't stir, just shake the saucepan occasionally, so the meat doesn't disintegrate. Simmer over a low heat for 10 minutes. If you want to make sure the sauce is substantial enough – if the meat has produced too much juice or the soured cream isn't thick enough – stir 1–2 tsp of flour into the soured cream before pouring it over the meat.
Place the chicken pieces into a warmed deep serving dish and cover them with the sauce. You could add a garnish of a few spots of soured cream, slices of cucumber, green pepper, tomato, or parsley, and accompany it with a lettuce salad.
To make the dumplings, break the eggs into the flour, add the salt, and gradually pour in enough milk to make a soft dough which doesn't drop easily from the spoon. Cut small dumplings from the dough into boiling salted water. As the dumplings rise to the surface, remove them with a draining spoon, rinse them with boiling water, and toss them in melted butter.

CHICKEN IN ALMOND BREADCRUMBS WITH POTATO SALAD
(Mandulás rántott csirke burgonyasalátával)

4	chicken drumsticks or 2 large boned breasts (4 fillets)
40 g (2 oz)	flour

Paprika chicken with dumplings

2	eggs
40 g (2 oz)	breadcrumbs
50 g (2½ oz)	almonds, peeled and coarsely chopped
1	lemon
	parsley
	salt
	oil for frying
	For the potato salad:
1 kg (2 lb)	potatoes
1	medium onion
4–5 tbsps	vinegar
1 tsp	mixture of salt and pepper
1–2 tbsps	caster sugar
2 tbsps	olive oil for the dressing

Wash the meat and wipe it dry (if using breasts, beat them out a little), sprinkle a little salt over each piece and leave to stand for 30 minutes. Beat the eggs, and combine the almonds and the breadcrumbs. Then coat the meat with the flour, then with the eggs, then with the breadcrumb mixture. Fry it in plenty of hot oil, then place it on a paper towel and garnish with slices of lemon and sprigs of parsley.
The potato salad should ideally be prepared the previous day, or at least 4–5 hours before serving. Wash the potatoes thoroughly and cook them unpeeled. Peel them while still hot and leave them to cool to room temperature, then slice them thinly into a deep bowl. Peel the onion, cut it into thin rings and scatter these over the potatoes. Bring 200 ml (7 fl oz) water to the boil with the vinegar, the salt and the sugar, and immediately pour it over the potatoes and onions, then shake the bowl gently to mix everything together. Leave the salad to cool completely. When serving, sprinkle the oil and some freshly-milled pepper on top.
Variations:
- Instead of the onion, chop a large bunch of chives and add this after the boiling water, when it has cooled a little.
- Cook a medium celeriac with the potatoes, then chop or slice it and add it to the potatoes.

DUCK STUFFED WITH CABBAGE PASTA (Káposztás kockával töltött kacsa)

1	roasting duck (about 1.5 kg / 3 lb)
	salt
1 tsp	crumbled marjoram
	For the stuffing:
400 g (14 oz)	white cabbage, grated
	salt and pepper
20 g (1 oz)	sugar
3 tbsps	oil
150 g (5 oz)	flat square pasta
2	eggs, beaten

Clean the duck thoroughly and remove the oil gland. Lay it on its breast, cut open the back and, using a very sharp small knife, cut the leg and wing joints and then remove the meat from the bones, taking care to leave the skin intact. Remove any excess fat from the cavity, sprinkle salt over it and then rub it with the marjoram.
Brown the sugar in the oil, then add the cabbage, and salt and pepper to taste, and fry it uncovered over a strong heat, stirring constantly. Cook the pasta in slightly salted water, then rinse it in cold water, drain it and add it to the cabbage, together with the eggs. Stir well, and pile the mixture onto the middle of the boned duck. Lift the two sides of the back and secure them with closely-spaced stitches. Place the duck on its breast in a baking tray, cover it with foil, and bake it in a preheated moderate oven (180°C / 350°F / gas mark 4) for 45–50 minutes, until tender. Then turn it over, place it on a wire rack in the baking tray, and return it to the oven, increasing the setting to hot until the duck is well browned. Leave it to stand for 15 minutes.
Remove the stitches before serving, then place the duck onto a warmed large serving dish, and carve it at the table. Serve with vegetables cooked in salted water and sprinkled with melted butter.
Note: Cabbage pasta (made without eggs) is a popular dish in Hungary, served as a second course after less substantial soups. It is generally eaten with a liberal sprinkling of pepper, though many people like to sprinkle it with sugar instead.

GOOSE HASH WITH GOOSE DRUMSTICKS (Ludaskása libacombbal)

4	medium goose drumsticks (or 2 breasts, or 1 kg / 2 lb giblets)
1	medium onion, peeled and left whole
	peppercorns
	salt
2	cloves garlic
400 g (14 oz)	mixed vegetables for soup (carrots, parsnips, celeriac, kohlrabi) peeled and chopped
200 g (7 oz)	long grain rice

Clean the meat carefully, place it in a saucepan with enough cold water to cover it, and bring to the boil. When the water boils, add the onion, 10–15 peppercorns and the garlic in an infuser, and a little salt, cover the pan, and simmer over a low heat. After 30 minutes, add the vegetables, and carry on simmering until the meat is tender but not yet coming away from the bone.
Carefully remove the goose drumsticks from the liquid, make criss-cross cuts in the skin, and roast them in the oven, basting occasionally with their own fat (or alternatively with a mixture of beer and honey) until the skin is browned and crisp. Keep warm.

Discard the onion and the contents of the infuser, skim the fat off the surface of the stock, then strain it. Layer the cooked vegetables with the rice in a heat-proof dish, add 600 ml (1 pint) of the hot stock, cover, and bake in a preheated moderate oven (180°C / 350°F / gas mark 4) until tender. Stir only once, halfway through the cooking time, or it will become sticky! If it is too dry, add a little more hot stock at this stage.

Leave the rice and vegetables in the baking dish or transfer them to a warmed serving dish, place the goose drumsticks on top, and serve immediately. Accompany with braised red cabbage, pickles, or a seasonal mixed salad.

Note:

- If you are using giblets, chop them before cooking, and add them to the rice at the same time as the vegetables.
- You could enrich the dish with 100 g (4 oz) peas and 100 g (4 oz) mushrooms; you don't need to pre-cook these, just add them to the rice with the other vegetables.

STUFFED ROAST GOOSE WITH BRAISED RED CABBAGE (Töltött libasült párolt vöröskáposztával)

Serves 8

1	roasting goose (3–3.5 kg / 6–7 lb)
	salt and pepper
1	large onion
2 tbsps	oil
4	apples
	juice of 1 lemon
4	bread rolls
300–400 ml	(½ – ¾ pint) milk
	the goose's liver (250–300 g / about 10 oz)
200 g (7 oz)	smoked raw ham or shoulder of pork
1	large bunch parsley, chopped
2	cloves garlic, crushed
2	eggs
50 ml (2 fl oz)	brandy
	For the braised red cabbage:
800 g (1¾ lb)	red cabbage

Goose hash with goose drumsticks

400 g (14 oz)	white cabbage
50 ml (2 fl oz)	oil or fat
1 tbsp	sugar
1	small onion, finely chopped
1 tsp	noble-sweet paprika
2 tbsps	vinegar or lemon juice
	salt, pepper, and caraway seeds

Clean the goose thoroughly, salt it inside and out, sprinkle a little pepper into the cavity, and leave it to stand for about 1 hour.
Prepare the stuffing: chop the onion finely and fry it in the oil until just softened, then leave it to cool; peel, core, and dice the apples, and sprinkle them immediately with a little lemon juice to prevent them going brown; soak the rolls in lukewarm milk, then squeeze them out thoroughly; and dice the goose liver and the ham very finely. Mix them all together, adding the parsley, the garlic, salt and pepper to taste, and the brandy. Stuff the mixture firmly into the cavity of the goose: any remainder can go into the neck cavity or under the skin on the breast. Stitch up the cavity with strong white thread, truss the legs, fold the wings underneath, and place the goose onto a rack in a baking tray (so it doesn't drown in its own fat). Pour a little water into the baking tray, cover the goose with foil, and place in a preheated hot oven (220°C / 425°F / gas mark 7). After 1 hour, remove the foil, and continue roasting, basting the goose with its own fat and juices, until it is well browned. Constantly remove the fat produced while the goose roasts, and cover the parts which brown quickly (legs, breast) with foil so they don't burn.
Leave the goose to stand for 10–15 minutes after roasting, then remove the thread and trussing string, and place it on a warmed serving dish. Garnish with lemon slices and parsley, and carve at the table. Serve with roast and mashed potatoes.
To make the braised red cabbage, wash the cabbages, cut them in half, remove the cores, and then shred them. Brown the sugar in the fat until golden, add the onion and fry it until softened, sprinkle the paprika on top, and then add 200 ml (7 fl oz) cold water with the vinegar. Stir in the grated cabbage, add salt and pepper to taste, flavour with caraway seeds, cover the pan, and braise over a low heat until tender.
Note: The cabbage will taste even better if prepared the previous day, but take care with the salt, as it will taste more salty after standing than when fresh.

MINCED GOOSE LIVER WITH APPLE PURÉE (Vagdalt libamell almapürével)

1	goose liver (about 1 kg / 2 lb)
2	dry bread rolls
400 ml (¾ pint)	milk
2 tbsps	oil
1	medium onion, finely chopped
100 g (4 oz)	mushrooms, chopped
2	eggs
2	cloves garlic, crushed
	grated rind and strained juice of 1 lemon
½ tsp	dried marjoram
1 bunch	parsley, chopped
	salt and pepper
	a few lettuce leaves
	For the apple purée:
1 kg (2 lb)	slightly tart apples
4–5 tbsps	lemon juice
1 tbsp	honey
250 ml (8 fl oz)	dry white wine
1	pinch salt

Remove the meat from the bone and mince it, together with the skin. Soak the rolls in the milk. Fry the onion in 1 tbsp of the oil until transparent, then add the mushrooms, fry together for a few minutes over a strong heat, and leave to cool completely. Squeeze out the rolls and add them to the meat, together with the cooled onion and mushroom mixture, eggs, garlic, lemon rind and juice, marjoram, parsley, and salt and pepper to taste, and work together thoroughly.
Grease a heatproof dish with the remaining oil, then divide the mince mixture into two and pile it back onto the bone, smoothing it to a rounded shape, and place it into the dish. Pour in 100 ml (4 fl oz) water, and roast in a preheated moderate oven (180°C / 350°F / gas mark 4) for 60–80 minutes, until nicely browned.
Meanwhile, *prepare the apple purée:* wash, peel and core the apples, cut them into 4–8 segments, and sprinkle them with the lemon juice so they don't go brown. Stir the honey into the wine and add the mixture to the apples, together with a pinch of salt, then cover the pan, and cook over a low heat for about 30 minutes, until the apples are soft and pulpy. Uncover the pan for the last 10 minutes to dry the purée out a little; keep it warm.
Remove the mince from the oven, cover it with foil, and leave it to stand for 15 minutes. Then loosen it with a knife and carefully remove it from the bone, slice it fairly thickly, and lay the slices back onto the bone, overlapping them slightly. Serve on an oblong dish, garnished with lettuce and parsley leaves. Serve the apple purée in a separate bowl.

MUTTON PÖRKÖLT (Birkapörkölt)

Serves 4–6

1 kg (2 lb)	leg or shoulder of mutton (boned)
100 g (4 oz)	lard or oil
150 g (5 oz)	onions
1 tsp	noble sweet paprika
1	green pepper
1	tomato

½	cherry paprika
2	cloves garlic, crushed
	ground caraway seeds
	salt

Carefully remove all the fat and membranes from the meat, wash it, and cut it into 3 cm (1 in) cubes. Scald the meat and drain it thoroughly (you don't need to do this if you are using lamb). Chop the onion finely and fry it in the fat until transparent, then remove from the heat and sprinkle on the paprika, and add the meat. Stir well, and fry over a strong heat, stirring constantly, until the meat whitens. Reduce the heat, add the green pepper, the tomato, the sharp paprika, the garlic, a pinch of caraway seeds, and salt to taste, then cover the pan, and braise the meat in its own juices over a moderate heat until tender. Serve with dumplings, tarhonya, or potatoes cooked in salted water and cut into chunks, accompanied with pickles.

Note: The authentic way to prepare this ancient shepherds' dish is in a cauldron over an open fire. There are several methods of cooking it in this way, some requiring considerable expertise and practice. The simplest is when all the ingredients are put into the cauldron together, with a little water, but the salt and paprika are only added halfway through the cooking time, and the caraway seeds and garlic may be omitted altogether. The important rule is not to keep stirring the food, but to twist and shake the cauldron occasionally to stop the meat catching.

Variation: This dish can also be made with pork or beef (leg or shoulder).

PORK

BLACK PUDDING AND SAUSAGE FEAST WITH ONION MASH (Disznótoros hagymás tört burgonyával)

Serves 4–6

1 kg (2 lb)	black puddings (or haggis)
400 g (14 oz)	fresh baking sausage (you can get these from continental food shops or delicatessens)
800 g (1¾ lb)	potatoes
50 g (2 oz)	oil or fat
1	large onion, thinly sliced
	salt and pepper

Wash the black puddings and lay them in a large baking tray or heatproof dish. Prick them in several places with a skewer. Add a little water (not fat!), and bake in a preheated medium oven (180°C / 350°F / gas mark 4) for 40–45 minutes. Halfway through the baking time, carefully turn the black puddings, place the sausage next to them, and return to the oven until they are all crisp.

The sausage can also be fried separately on the hob: put it in a small pan, add a little water, cover the pan, and braise it for 20 minutes. Turn the sausage occasionally, but be careful not to pierce the skin, as the juices will be lost and it will be too dry. Finally, remove the lid and fry it until its fat melts.

While the black pudding is in the oven, prepare *the onion mash.* Cook the potatoes unpeeled, then peel them while still hot and mash them roughly with a fork, or cut them into thin slices or small cubes. Fry the onion in the fat until softened, add the potato, and stir vigorously, breaking it up even more. Add salt and pepper to taste, and heat it up over a moderate heat until the bottom layer is crisp.

Leave the black puddings in the baking dish or arrange them onto a warmed serving dish and serve with the onion mash, accompanied with braised red cabbage and pickles.

Note: The *disznótor* is the feast which follows the killing and processing of a fattened pig – a major event in Hungarian village life, involving a whole day of hard work to provide the family with a store of meat and meat products. Everyone who lends a hand receives some of the delicacies which result, including the black pudding and sausage used in this recipe.

Black pudding and sausage feast with onion mash

ÓVÁR PORK CHOPS (Óvári sertésborda)

4	pork chops (600 g / 1¼lb)
	salt and pepper
100 g (4 oz)	flour
100 g (4 oz)	butter or margarine
5 tbsps	oil
300 g (11 oz)	mushrooms, sliced
8 slices	ham
8 slices	half fat cheese
200 ml (7 fl oz)	semi-dry red wine

Beat out the meat a little, then salt it and leave to stand for 30 minutes. Heat the butter and the oil together, coat the chops with the flour, fry them quickly on both sides, then lay them in a baking tray. Fry the mushrooms in the remaining fat, then remove the pan from the heat, add salt and pepper, and distribute the mushrooms equally over the chops. Then cover each with a slice of ham and a slice of cheese, and bake in a preheated hot oven (220°C / 425°F / gas mark 7) only until the cheese melts and browns a little.

Skim the fat off the meat juices, pour in the wine, and boil until the liquid is reduced to half its original volume. Strain it, and serve it in a separate bowl.

Accompany with braised vegetables tossed in butter, or rice mixed with peas.

VINE-DRESSER'S PORK CHOPS (Sertésborda vincellér módra)

4	pork chops
	salt
2–3 tbsps	flour
30 g (1 oz)	butter
2 tbsps	oil
	pepper
200 ml (7 fl oz)	semi-dry white wine
1	bay leaf
800 g (1¾ lb)	dessert grapes
30 ml (1 fl oz)	cognac
	For the sauce:
30 g (1 oz)	butter
1 tbsp	sugar
2 tbsps	wine vinegar
400ml (¾ pint)	full bodied red wine
	salt
1 tbsp	arrowroot

Beat the meat out a little, salt it, and leave it to stand for 30 minutes, then wipe it dry and coat it with the flour. Heat the butter with the oil, and quickly fry the meat on both sides. Scatter a little freshly-milled pepper on top, pour in the wine, and add the bay leaf. Cover the pan, and braise the meat, turning it occasionally, until tender. Then remove the lid and reduce the liquid until hardly any remains. Wash the grapes and remove the stalks, add them to the meat, and braise for a few minutes. Don't stir, just shake the pan occasionally. Remove from the heat, pour on the cognac, cover the pan, and leave to stand for a few minutes.

Meanwhile, *prepare the sauce:* brown the sugar in the butter, pour in the wine vinegar and the wine, add a little salt, and boil over a strong heat, without covering the pan, until the liquid is reduced by half. Stir the arrowroot into 2–3 tbsps cold water and stir the mixture into the sauce. Return to the boil only briefly until it thickens.

Lay the chops onto a warmed serving dish and pile the grapes around them. Strain the meat juices into the sauce and stir vigorously. Use some of the sauce to coat the chops, and pour the rest over the grapes or serve in a separate warmed bowl.

STUFFED LOIN OF PORK CSABA STYLE (Csabai töltött karaj)

Serves 6–8

1.2 kg (2½ lb)	loin of pork, boned, in one piece
	salt and pepper
1 stick	(250 g / 9 oz) smoked ("Csabai") paprika sausage
	salt and pepper
3	large onions
6	cloves garlic
1	level tsp caraway seeds
4 tbsps	oil
250 ml (8 fl oz)	dry white wine

Rinse the meat, salt it and leave it to stand for 30 minutes, then wipe it dry. Using a thin bladed knife, cut a slit through the middle of the joint. Wash the sausage and insert it into the slit. Place the joint into a deep baking tray, brush it with the oil, and rub in a little freshly-milled pepper and the caraway seeds. Peel the onions and the garlic, cut the onions into segments, and add both to the meat, then pour in the wine, cover with foil, and bake in a moderate oven (180°C / 350°F / gas mark 4) for 1 hour.

Remove the foil from the meat, raise the oven setting to 220°C / 425°F / gas mark 7, and return the meat to the oven for 25–30 minutes, basting it with its own juices, until it is browned on all sides. Lift the meat out of the juices, cover it with foil, and leave it to stand for 10 minutes. Slice the meat fairly thickly and arrange the slices on a serving dish, sprinkle on a little of the juices, and garnish with slices of cucumber or lettuce leaves. Serve the onion and garlic braised in the meat juices in a separate bowl (they will be very popular). Accompany with chips or roast potatoes.

Stuffed loin of pork Csaba style

Note: This dish is also very decorative and tastes just as good when cold, and is an important component of a cold buffet. Leave the meat to cool and then slice it thinly. Arrange the slices on a large dish, overlapping slightly, and until it is time to serve, make an airtight cover over the dish with clingfilm, or brush a wafer-thin coating of aspic over the slices, otherwise they will dry out and discolour, which will make them unappetising.
Accompany with a salad of potatoes and onions or other cooked vegetables dressed with mayonnaise, or a cabbage salad with onions, or mixed pickles.

PORK CHOPS WITH POTATOES AND LECSÓ (Lecsós-burgonyás sertésborda)

8	pork chops
	salt and pepper
2–3 tbsps	flour
	oil for frying
600 g (1¼lb)	potatoes
50 g (2 oz)	smoked streaky bacon
1	medium onion
250 g (9 oz)	tomatoes
250 g (9 oz)	green peppers
½ tsp	slightly sharp paprika
1	clove garlic, crushed
	a few sprigs parsley

Wash the chops, salt them, and leave them to stand for 30 minutes. Then wipe them dry and coat them with the flour. Heat the oil and fry the chops quickly on both sides.
Wash the potatoes and cook them unpeeled, then peel them while still warm and leave them to cool.
Prepare the lecsó: cube the bacon and fry it until the fat melts; chop the onion finely and fry it in the bacon fat until just softened. Meanwhile, scald the tomatoes, peel them, and cut them into segments; and core and slice the green peppers. Sprinkle the paprika over the onions, add the tomatoes, and boil for a few minutes uncovered, then add the green peppers, garlic, and salt and pepper to taste, cover the pan, and braise under a moderate heat until not quite softened.
Use the oil in which the chops were fried to grease a deep heatproof dish. Slice the potatoes and spread the slices over the bottom of the dish, and sprinkle on a little salt. Arrange the chops on top, and spread the lecsó smoothly over the chops. Place in a preheated oven (180°C / 350°F / gas mark 4) for 15–20 minutes, until it is piping hot throughout. Serve in the same dish, garnished with parsley.
Variation: This is also excellent when made with veal cutlets, or turkey or chicken breasts.
Note: This is a good Hungarian-style dish, the best of it being the potatoes which absorb the flavours. It is also a good dish to prepare in advance when you are expecting guests.

TEMESVÁR PORK CHOPS WITH GREEN BEANS (Temesvári sertésborda zöldbabbal)

8	pork chops on the bone
	salt
100 g (4 oz)	flour
100 ml (4 fl oz)	oil
1	large onion
2 tsps	paprika
2	cloves garlic, crushed
600 g (1¼lb)	potatoes
2	green peppers, cored and thinly sliced
2	tomatoes, peeled and chopped
40 g (2 oz)	flour
400ml (¾ pint)	soured cream
	a few tomato slices
1	bunch parsley
	For the accompaniment:
500 g (1 lb)	green beans
	salt
2	cloves garlic
8–10	thin slices smoked bacon

Beat the chops gently, salt them and leave them to stand for 30 minutes, then coat them with the flour, heat the oil, and fry them on both sides until browned. Transfer them to a large saucepan.
Chop the onion finely and fry it in the oil until just softened, then add the paprika and the garlic. Pour on 200 ml (7 fl oz) water, add salt, and boil for a few minutes over a strong heat, then pour it onto the meat. Cover the pan, and braise the meat over a moderate heat until tender, then remove the meat from the liquid and keep it warm.
Peel and slice the potatoes, and put them into the liquid, together with the green peppers and tomatoes. Add enough water to just cover them, then cover the pan and cook until almost softened. Stir the flour into the soured cream and use the mixture to thicken the liquid, then check the seasoning, return the meat to the saucepan, and simmer over a low heat for another 5 minutes.
While the potatoes are cooking, cook the green beans in salted water, with the garlic, until soft. Drain the beans and cut the ends so that they are all the same length, then wrap the beans in the bacon slices, 5 or 6 beans per slice, place them on a baking tray, and bake in a preheated hot oven (220°C / 425°F / gas mark 7) for 5 minutes.
Spread the potatoes in the bottom of a serving dish using a slotted spoon, lay the chops on top of the potatoes or at the side of the dish, place the bacon-wrapped bunches of beans all around, splash on the soured cream sauce, and garnish with tomato slices and

chopped parsley. Serve hot, with extra soured cream on the side.

PORK BAKONY STYLE (Szűzérmék bakonyi módra)

4	fillet steaks (250 g / 9 oz each)
	salt and pepper
250 g (9 oz)	mushrooms
1	green pepper
1	tomato
50 ml (2 fl oz)	oil
1 tbsp	margarine
4–5 tbsps	flour
1	large onion
1 tsp	noble-sweet paprika
200 ml (7 fl oz)	soured cream
	a few sprigs of parsley, chopped

Remove the membranes from the meat, wash and salt it and leave it to stand for 30 minutes. Wipe the mushrooms with a coarse cotton cloth. Cut off just the dirty ends of the stalks, and slice the mushrooms fairly thickly. Wash the green pepper and the tomato; cut the green pepper into rings, and peel the tomato and cut it into segments.

Heat the oil and margarine in a frying pan. Wipe the meat dry, coat each piece with flour, and seal it quickly on both sides, then transfer to a large saucepan. Chop the onion finely and braise it in the remaining fat. Add the mushrooms, green pepper and tomato, and fry over a strong heat for 3–4 minutes. Add the paprika, pour on 100 ml (4 fl oz) water, and add salt and freshly-milled pepper to taste. Bring to the boil, and pour over the meat. Cover the pan, and braise the meat over a moderate heat for 25–30 minutes until tender (if the liquid evaoprates, replace it with a little water). Finally, set aside 1 tbsp of the soured cream, then stir 1 tsp of flour into the remainder, add it to the sauce, and return to the boil for a few minutes.

Put the meat onto a chopping board and cut it into oblique slices. Arrange the slices on a serving dish and spoon the sauce beside them. Put a few spots of

Pork Bakony style

the reserved soured cream onto the sauce, and put a few drops of the red fat from the top of the sauce in the middle of the soured cream spots. Pull a knife tip through each to make a pattern, and garnish with a few pinches of the chopped parsley.
This dish should be served with dumplings, but a good alternative is rice mixed with parsley or peas.
Note: Anything made in Bakony style is a *paprikás* with mushrooms and soured cream or single cream added to the sauce.

ŐRSÉG GRILL WITH MUSHROOMS (Őrségi gombás flekken)

200g (7 oz)	mushrooms – various types
1	sprig fresh (or 1 tsp dried) thyme
8	small slices leg or shoulder of pork (about 1 kg / 2 lb)
	salt and pepper
100 ml (4 fl oz)	oil
100 ml (4 fl oz)	full-bodied red wine

Wipe the mushrooms thoroughly with a coarse cotton cloth, remove any dirt, and slice them fairly thickly. Wash the thyme and remove the leaves. Wash the meat and wipe it dry with a paper towel, then beat it out gently.
Put 1 tbsp oil into a dish with a close-fitting lid, coat a piece of meat with oil and then sprinkle it with salt and pepper to taste, season with some thyme, and put 4 or 5 mushroom slices on top. Put the next piece of meat on top of that, add the seasoning and mushrooms as above, and repeat until all the ingredients are used. Pour on the remaining oil, and the wine, cover the dish, and leave it in the refrigerator overnight.
The next day, take the meat out of the refrigerator 30 minutes before cooking it. Preheat the oven to 180°C / 350°F / gas mark 4. Use half the marinade to grease a heatproof dish. Lay the meat slices together with the mushrooms into the dish, pour on the remaining marinade, cover the dish, and bake in the oven for about 45 minutes. Remove the cover, and return to the oven for 15 minutes until browned. Serve in the same dish; you could add a garnish of chopped parsley. Accompany with roast potatoes or croquette potatoes and braised vegetables.
Note:
- you can also use dried mushrooms, but then you only need one tenth of the amount, i.e. 20 g / ¾ oz;
- this dish tastes even better when barbecued, but then it's better to fry the mushrooms in a separate pan, otherwise they could easily burn or fall through the barbecue grill.

TORDA BARBECUE WITH CABBAGE AND DILL (Tordai lacipecsenye kapros káposztával)

4	thick pork chops with rind (800 g / 1¾ lb)
	salt
1 kg / 2 lb	white cabbage
1	large bunch dill
1	large onion
50 g (2 oz)	smoked streaky bacon
200 ml (7 fl oz)	oil
2 tsps	paprika
2	cloves garlic, crushed
200 ml (7 fl oz)	soured cream
100 g (4 oz)	flour

Beat out the chops a little, and with a sharp knife cut slits 1 cm (½ in) apart in the rind. Salt the chops and leave them to stand for 30 minutes.
Remove the core of the cabbage and cut the leaves into 1 cm (½ in) wide strips; chop the dill and finely chop the onion. Cube the bacon and fry it in 2 tbsps oil until the fat melts, then fry the onion until just softened. Add half the dill, then remove the pan from the heat and stir in the paprika and the cabbage. Add the garlic, and salt to taste, then cover the pan, and braise the cabbage in its own juices over a moderate heat until softened. Stir 2 tbsps flour into the soured cream and pour this onto the cabbage. Simmer for a few minutes, then scatter the remaining dill on top and keep warm.
Heat the remaining oil. Combine the remaining flour with 1 tsp paprika, and coat each chop with the mixture. Shake off the excess, and fry the chops in the oil until browned on both sides. Arrange the chops on a warmed serving dish, spoon the cabbage around them, and serve hot, with extra soured cream in a separate bowl.
Note: The cabbage can be prepared in advance; it reheats well.

WHEELWRIGHT'S ROAST (STUFFED PORK BELLY) (Bognárpecsenye or töltött sertésoldalas)

800 g (1¾ lb)	lean pork belly, boned
	salt and pepper
150 g (5 oz)	minced pork shoulder
150 g (5 oz)	pig's liver
5	cloves garlic, 1 crushed
1	egg
½ tsp	paprika
1 pinch	marjoram
1	large onion, peeled and quartered
1 tsp	caraway seeds
100 ml (4 fl oz)	dry white wine

Make a slit in the meat for the stuffing, and rub it with salt and pepper inside and out.
For the stuffing: dice the liver and add it to the mince, together with the crushed garlic, the egg, paprika, and marjoram. Work together well, and stuff the meat with the mixture, then secure the opening with closely-spaced stitches. Place the meat in a large saucepan, together with the onion and the remaining 4 cloves of garlic. Scatter the caraway seeds on top, pour in the wine, cover the pan, and braise the meat over a low heat until almost tender. Transfer it to a deep baking tray (or use the saucepan, if it is ovenproof: bakelite handles aren't!), pour on the juices, and roast in a preheated hot oven (220°C / 425°F / gas mark 7) for 25–30 minutes until browned, basting frequently. Leave it to stand for 10 minutes before slicing and serving, so the stuffing doesn't fall apart. Serve with potatoes fried on their own or with onions, and a mixed salad. This is also excellent eaten cold, accompanied with some potato salad made with onions and parsley.
Note: This dish can also be made with veal breast.

PORK PLAIT WITH ALMONDS AND QUINCES (Sertésfonat – mandulás birsalmával)

4	thick leg or fillet steaks (800g / 1¾ lb)
	salt
1	sprig savory, finely chopped
4–5 tbsps	oil
1 kg (2 lb)	quinces
	rind and juice of 1 lemon
1 tbsp	honey
2 cm / 1 in	cinnamon stick
5–6	cloves
50 g (2 oz)	almonds, peeled and flaked
2–3	sprigs parsley, chopped
	a few lettuce leaves

Salt the meat and leave it to stand for 1 hour, then cut each steak lengthways into 3 equal strips, leaving them joined at one end. Plait each steak and secure the end with a skewer. Heat the oil in a frying pan and seal each meat plait on both sides, then transfer them to a baking tray, pour in a little water, and roast in a medium oven (180°C / 350°F / gas mark 4) until browned and tender.
Peel the quinces and cut them into segments, then immediately put them into water mixed with lemon juice so they don't go brown. Add the honey, cinnamon, cloves, 2 strips of lemon rind, and a pinch of salt, and cook until the quinces are tender, but not disintegrating. Lift them from the liquid with a slotted spoon and drain them. Roast the almond flakes in a non-stick frying pan (without fat), stirring constantly.

Pork plait with almonds and quinces

Arrange the meat plaits on a warmed serving dish, pile the quinces next to them, and scatter the almond flakes over the top. Garnish with a few pinches of chopped parsley and lettuce leaves. A sure-fire success!

PORK BRASSÓ STYLE (Brassói sertés aprópecsenye)

600 g (1¼lb)	pork fillet or leg
100 g (4 oz)	smoked bacon
2	medium onions
4	cloves garlic
	salt and pepper
	marjoram

Wash the meat and wipe it dry, then cut it into strips 2–3 cm (1 in) by 4–5 cm (2 inches). Cut the bacon into thin strips and fry it. Peel the onions and cut them into rings, and chop the garlic. Add both to the bacon, cover the pan, and fry until softened. Add the meat and fry over a strong heat for 5 minutes, then add salt to taste and a good sprinkling of pepper, and season with marjoram. Cover the pan, and braise the meat over a moderate heat until tender (if the meat juices evaporate, replace them with a little hot water or stock). Finally, fry the meat until the fat melts, check the seasoning, and pile it onto a warmed serving dish. Serve with fried potatoes, peas, and mixed salad.

Pork with prunes in red wine

PORK WITH PRUNES IN RED WINE (Malaccomb vörösboros aszalt szilvával)

	Serves 8
400 g (14 oz)	prunes, stoned
300 ml (½ pint)	red wine
1	leg joint with rind (about 2.5 kg / 5 lb including the bone)
	salt
2 tbsps	oil
1	large onion, peeled and sliced
4–5	cloves garlic
100 ml (4 fl oz)	beer
50 g (2 oz)	smoked bacon
1 tbsp	arrowroot

Soak the prunes overnight in the red wine. Salt the rindless surface of the meat and leave it to stand for 1 hour, then lay it rind down in a deep baking tray. Brush it with the oil, pour 100 ml (4 fl oz) water into the tray, and add the onion and garlic. Cover with foil and roast in a preheated oven (180°C / 350°F / gas mark 4) for 1 hour.

Turn the meat over and score the rind with a sharp knife. Wrap the end of the bone in foil so it doesn't burn, then return it to the oven. Baste it every 10–15 minutes with the bacon dipped in the beer, this will make it nice and crisp. If any blisters form, pierce them with a skewer, and replace the evaporated juices with a little water. Continue roasting for 2½ hours until browned and crisp.

Place the meat on an oblong dish and leave it to stand for 10–15 minutes; remove the foil from the bone. Strain the juices into a small saucepan and skim off the fat. Add the prunes and wine, and bring to the boil. Stir the arrowroot into 3 tbsps cold water, add it to the boiling liquid, and return to the boil briefly. Carve some of the meat, arrange the slices on a serving dish, and serve with the prunes. Accompany with mashed potatoes.

Note: It's not worth reheating any left-over meat, because the rind will go soggy; it's better to eat it cold, accompanied with pickles or preserves.

BUTCHER'S STEW WITH TARHONYA (Hentestokány tarhonyával)

600 g (1¼lb)	shoulder or leg of pork
150 g (5 oz)	bacon
50 g (2 oz)	oil or lard
1	large onion, finely chopped
2	cloves garlic, chopped
1 tbsp	tomato purée
100 ml (4 fl oz)	semi-dry white wine
	salt and pepper
200 g (7 oz)	pickled gherkins
200 ml (7 fl oz)	single cream
	For the tarhonya:
250 g (9 oz)	dried *tarhonya*
50 g (2 oz)	fat (butter, oil, or fat)
1	medium onion, finely chopped or grated
	salt

Wash the meat and wipe it dry, then cut it into long strips 1.5 cm (½ in) wide. Cut the bacon into strips as well, add the fat and fry it a little, then add the onion and fry it until transparent. Add the garlic, tomato purée, and wine, and bring to the boil.

Stir in the meat strips, add salt to taste and a good sprinkling of pepper, then cover the pan, and braise the meat over a low heat until tender, replacing any evaporated juices with a little water. Cut the gherkins into thin strips or grate them coarsely, add them to the meat, and braise for another 5 minutes. Finally, pour in the cream, boil for 4–5 minutes until thickened, and check the seasoning.

Place the stew onto a warmed serving dish, and serve with tarhonya or potatoes cooked in salted water and tossed in parsley butter.

To prepare the tarhonya, heat the fat, then add the tarhonya, and fry it uncovered over a low heat, stirring constantly, until it turns pale. Add the onion, fry for a few more minutes, then pour on enough boiling water to cover it amply, add salt, and give it a stir. Cover the pan, and cook over a low heat (or preferably in the oven), replacing any evaporated liquid with a little boiling water. Don't stir, just give the saucepan a shake, otherwise the tarhonya will become sticky. When it has softned, loosen it with a fork and serve.

Note: *Tarhonya* is a Hungarian speciality, a type of dried pasta which can be made at home or bought ready-made. To make your own, you need 100 g (4 oz) flour, 1 egg, a little water, and salt. Knead into a firm dough, then press it through a large coarse-meshed sieve to form small dumplings similar to *csipetke*.

VEAL AND BEEF

STUFFED VEAL BREAST (Töltött borjúszegy)

800 g (1¾ lb)	boned veal breast (or use lean pork belly)
	salt and pepper
200 ml (7 fl oz)	milk
4	dry bread rolls
2	medium onions
1	large bunch parsley
200 g (7 oz)	mushrooms
50 g (2 oz)	lean smoked bacon
1 tbsp	butter or margarine
4	eggs
4 tbsps	oil
100 ml (4 fl oz)	dry white wine
1 tbsp	tomato purée
1 tbsp	flour
	a few lettuce leaves

Carefully cut a slit in the meat without puncturing it (mend any holes with closely-spaced stitches using thin thread), and salt it inside and out. Dilute the milk with 200 ml (7 fl oz) warm water and pour it onto the rolls. Peel and wipe the vegetables as appropriate, and chop the onion and the parsley finely, dice the mushrooms, and also the bacon. Set aside 1 tbsp of the chopped parsley for the sauce.

Heat the butter and fry the bacon, add the onions and mushrooms, and continue frying, uncovered, for 5 minutes, then leave to cool to room temperature.

Stuffed veal breast

Squeeze the rolls out thoroughly and add them to the onion and mushroom mixture, together with the eggs and parsley. Add salt and pepper to taste, and stir well. Stuff the meat with the mixture, stitch up the opening, and place the meat onto a baking tray.
Heat the oil, pour it over the meat, and roast it in a hot oven for 10 minutes. Reduce the heat to 180°C / 350°F / gas mark 4, pour in the wine, and roast the meat for about 1 hour, basting occasionally with its juices, until well browned. Place the meat onto a board and leave it to stand for 10 minutes.
Meanwhile, prepare the sauce: skim the fat off the surface of the meat juices, strain them, stir in the tomato purée, and bring to the boil. Stir the flour into 50 ml / 2 fl oz water until smooth and add the mixture to the sauce, season with salt and pepper, boil for 2 minutes, and finally stir in the reserved parsley.
Remove the thread from the meat and slice it fairly thickly. Arrange the slices on a warmed serving dish and garnish with the lettuce leaves. Pour a little of the sauce onto and around the meat and serve the rest in a separate bowl. Serve with chips or mashed potatoes or boiled rice.
Variations:
- use lean pork belly instead of veal;
- replace the mushrooms in the stuffing with a little diced ham or liver or apple.

VEAL KEDVESSY STYLE (Borjúszelet Kedvessy módra)

4	veal fillet steaks (600 g / 1¼lb)
150 g (5 oz)	raw goose liver
150 g (5 oz)	calf's kidneys, cleaned
4	large mushroom heads
	salt and pepper
30 g (1 oz)	butter
1	large onion
1 tsp	sweet paprika
1	green pepper, chopped
1	tomato, chopped
100 g (4 oz)	flour
200 ml (7 fl oz)	soured cream
100 ml (4 fl oz)	single cream, beaten
1	large bunch dill, finely chopped
100 ml (4 fl oz)	oil and 100 g (4 oz) butter or margarine

Beat out the meat slightly. Cut the goose liver and the kidney into 4 slices or strips, and salt them, together with the mushrooms.
For the sauce, chop the onion finely and fry it in the butter until just softened. Sprinkle on the paprika, pour on 100 ml (4 fl oz) water, add the green pepper and tomato, and season with salt and pepper. Cover the pan, and simmer for 15 minutes. Stir 1 tbsp of the flour into the soured cream and use the mixture to thicken the sauce; return to the boil, and simmer for a few minutes. Strain the sauce, stir in the cream and the dill, and return to the boil briefly.
Coat the meat, the goose liver, the kidney, and the mushrooms with the remaining flour, and shake off the excess. Heat the oil and butter mixture, and fry the meat and mushrooms quickly. Make piles of veal – goose liver – kidney – mushroom on a warmed serving dish, pour on the hot dill and paprika sauce, and serve immediately.
Note: This dish is named after the master chef Nándor Kedvessy, who became famous for his French-style cooking.

MEAT LOAF WITH GRAPES (Kívül-belül szőlős fasírt)

800 g (1¾ lb)	large white dessert grapes
50 ml (2 fl oz)	brandy (cognac)
2 tbsps	butter or margarine
4 tbsps	breadcrumbs
100 g (4 oz)	pig's or calf's liver
1	small onion
500 g (1 lb)	minced topside or silverside
2	eggs
40 g (1½oz)	grated parmesan cheese
	ground nutmeg
	salt and pepper
2 tbsps	oil
100 ml (4 fl oz)	semi-sweet white wine

Meat loaf with grapes

Wash the grapes thoroughly, removing the stalks, and dry them with a tea towel. Cut 20–25 grapes in half with a sharp knife, remove the pips, pour the brandy over them and leave for 15 minutes.
Use half the butter to grease an oblong loaf tin and sprinkle it with breadcrumbs. Dice the liver; peel, wash, and grate the onion. Combine the mince, liver, onion, eggs, grated cheese, grapes and brandy, and the remaining breadcrumbs. Season with a pinch of nutmeg and salt and pepper, and work together well. With wet hands form the mixture into a sausage shape, and place it in the loaf tin. Brush the top with the oil and bake it in the oven (180°C / 350°F / gas mark 4) for about 1 hour until nicely browned. Remove the loaf from the tin, place it on a board, cover it with foil, and leave it to stand for 10 minutes. Meanwhile, heat the remaining butter in a medium-sized frying pan, add the remaining grapes, and fry for 2–3 minutes, shaking the pan constantly. Pour in the wine, season with a pinch of salt, then lower the heat, cover the pan, and braise for 5 minutes.
Slice the meat loaf fairly thickly, arrange the slices on a warmed serving dish, and surround them with the braised grapes. Serve with mashed potatoes.

STUFFED SIRLOIN SZEKSZÁRD STYLE (Szekszárdi töltött hátszín)

4	boned sirloin steaks (about 800 g / 1¾ lb)
	salt and pepper
200 ml (7 fl oz)	full-bodied red wine
15–20	prunes
200 ml (7 fl oz)	milk
2	dry bread rolls
6 tbsps	oil
2	medium onions, finely chopped
100 g (4 oz)	chicken or turkey liver, chopped
100 g (4 oz)	mushrooms, chopped
8–10	celery leaves, chopped
1	egg
½ tsp	crumbled marjoram
500 ml (1 pint)	meat stock (made with stock cube)
200 g (7 oz)	mixture of carrots and parsnips, chopped
100 g (4 oz)	tomato purée
2	cloves garlic, crushed
1	bay leaf
	grated rind and juice of ½ lemon
1 tsp	mustard
30 g (1 oz)	sugar
50 g (2 oz)	flour

Beat out the meat until it is nice and thin, and sprinkle it with salt and pepper. Soak the prunes in the red wine and the bread rolls in the milk. Peel the vegetables.
Prepare the stuffing: fry the onions in 4 tbsps of the oil until transparent. Transfer half (together with half the fat) into another saucepan and set aside. Add the liver, mushrooms, and celery leaves to the remainder, and fry for a few minutes over a strong heat, then leave to cool to room temperature. Squeeze out the rolls and add them to the liver mixture, together with the egg, the marjoram, and salt and pepper to taste, and work together well. Pile equal amounts of the mixture onto the middle of each steak, then roll up the steaks and secure them with thin string. Heat the oil and seal the meat on all sides, then pour in 200 ml (7 fl oz) of the stock, cover the pan, and braise the meat until tender.
Prepare the sauce: add the carrots and parsnips to the remaining fried onion and fry them together. Add the tomato purée, garlic, bay leaf, lemon rind and juice, mustard, and salt and pepper to taste. Pour in the remaining stock, cover the pan, and cook until the vegetables are tender, then press the sauce through a sieve while still warm. Brown the flour and sugar in the remaining oil. Pour on 100 ml (4 fl oz) cold water and stir until smooth, then drain the prunes and pour the red wine into the sauce. Simmer for a few minutes, and check the seasoning.
Cut the meat rolls into oblique slices and arrange them on a serving dish. Cover them with the sauce and surround them with the prunes. Serve with croquettes or mashed potatoes.

STEAK ESTERHÁZY (Esterházy rostélyos)

4	boned sirloin steaks (about 800 g / 1¾ lb)
	salt and pepper
50 g (2 oz)	butter or margarine
1	large onion
400 g (14 oz)	mixed vegetables (carrots, parsnips, kohlrabi, celeriac)
1	lemon
1	bay leaf
30 g (1 oz)	flour
200 ml (7 fl oz)	white wine
8–10	capers, chopped
200 ml (7 fl oz)	soured cream
1 tsp	mustard
1	level tsp caster sugar
2–3	sprigs parsley, chopped

Wash and dry the meat, beat each steak out a little, and sprinkle it with salt and pepper. Heat just over half the butter in a large saucepan and seal the steaks on both sides, then set aside. Peel and slice the onion, and fry it in the butter together with half the mixed vegetables. Sprinkle on the flour and pour in the wine and 100 ml (4 fl oz) water. Return the steaks to the saucepan, add the bay leaf, 2 strips of lemon rind, and salt and pepper to taste, then cover the pan and braise the meat over a low heat until tender, giving the saucepan an occasional shake.
Meanwhile, cut the remaining vegetables into thin strips. Heat the remaining butter or margarine and

fry the vegetables briefly, then pour in a little water, cover the pan, and braise the vegetables until tender. Arrange the steaks on a warmed serving dish and keep them warm. Strain the sauce into a small saucepan (just squeeze gently, don't force everything through the sieve), add the chopped capers, the braised vegetables, the sugar, and the soured cream. Simmer for a few minutes, then sharpen with the mustard and with lemon juice if necessary, and check the seasoning. Cover the meat slices with the sauce, sprinkle with the parsley, and serve hot with macaroni, bread dumplings, or boiled rice.

COWBOY STEAKS WITH POTATO NESTS (Csikós rostélyos burgonyafészekkel)

4	sirloin steaks
5 tbsps	oil or lard
60 g (2½ oz)	smoked bacon
1	large onion, diced
1–2	cloves garlic, crushed
1 tsp	noble-sweet paprika
	salt and pepper
200 g (7 oz)	green peppers
150 g (5 oz)	tomatoes
20 g (¾ oz)	flour
300 ml (½ pint)	soured cream
500 g (1 lb)	potatoes
20 g (¾ oz)	butter
100 ml (4 fl oz)	hot milk
2	sprigs parsley

Cowboy steaks with potato nests

Wash the meat, beat it out a little, and wipe it dry. Heat the fat in a frying pan and seal the meat quickly on both sides, then transfer it to a large saucepan. Cut the bacon into thin strips and fry it in the remaining fat. Add the onion and the garlic and fry until softened, then sprinkle on the paprika, pour on 200 ml (7 fl oz) water, and season with salt and pepper. Bring to the boil, and pour onto the meat. Cover the pan, and braise the meat over a low heat until almost tender, replacing any evaporated liquid with a little boiling water.
Core the green peppers and peel the tomatoes, chop both, and add them to the meat. Continue braising until tender. Finally, stir the flour into the soured cream, add the mixture to the meat, simmer for a few minutes, and check the seasoning.
After adding the green peppers and tomatoes to the meat, peel and dice the potatoes, and cook them in salted water until soft. Drain and mash them, then add the butter, ½ tsp salt, and the hot milk, and beat until creamy; keep warm.
To serve, put the mashed potato into a piping bag fitted with a star-shaped nozzle and pipe 8 neat nests onto a large flat serving dish. Arrange the steaks on the dish, and use a slotted spoon to take the bacon and vegetable mixture out of the sauce and place it in the nests. Spoon the remaining sauce around the nests, garnish with parsley leaves, and serve hot. You could also serve additional accompaniments of dumplings or boiled rice.
Note: You could make this dish with pork chops, turkey or chicken breasts, instead of beef.

STEAK WITH ONIONS (Hagymás rostélyos)

4	boned sirloin steaks (about 800 g / 1¾ lb)
	salt and pepper
200 g (7 oz)	oil
200 g (7 oz)	medium onions
150–200 g	(6–7 oz) flour

Wash and dry the steaks, cut slits all round the edges of each, beat them out nice and thin, and sprinkle them with a little salt and pepper. Put the steaks in a china or glass bowl, pour on 2–3 tbsps oil, cover, and refrigerate for at least 4–5 hours (or better still, for 2–3 days), turning the steaks frequently. If the meat is not marinated, it will be tough and chewy.
When you are ready to fry the steaks, first peel and slice the onions, separating the rings. Sprinkle them with salt and plenty of flour, and shake off the excess. Heat the oil and fry the onions, stirring gently, until

they are golden brown and crisp. Place the onion rings onto a paper towel, spreading them out so they stay crisp, and keep them warm.
Coat the meat slices with the remaining flour, and fry them uncovered in the oil until browned on both sides. Arrange the slices on a warmed serving dish, scatter the onion rings on top and all around, and serve immediately. Serve with potatoes fried with onions (see p. 33) and with mustard in a separate bowl.

STUFFED STEAK CSÁKY STYLE (Csáky töltött rostélyos)

4	boned sirloin steaks (800 g / 1¾ lb)
	salt and pepper
50 g (2 oz)	smoked streaky bacon
2	medium onions
500 g (1 lb)	green peppers
200 g (7 oz)	tomatoes
2 tsps	paprika
4	eggs
80 g (3 oz)	fat or oil
200 ml (7 fl oz)	soured cream
1 tsp	flour
	a few sprigs parsley
1	green pepper
1	tomato

Beat out the steaks a little, salt them, and leave to stand for 30 minutes. Prepare a lecsó: chop the onions finely; core and slice the green pepper; and peel and chop the tomato. Dice the bacon and fry it until the fat melts, then fry half the onion in the bacon fat until just softened. Sprinkle on 1 tsp paprika, add half the green pepper and tomato, add salt, and braise until tender. Beat the eggs with a little pepper, stir them into the lecsó and fry into a firm omelette, then leave it to cool. Put equal amounts onto each steak. Roll up each steak and secure with thin string, then heat the oil and fry each roll quickly. Remove the meat from the fat, then fry the remaining onion in it until transparent. Sprinkle on the remaining paprika, pour on 200 ml (7 fl oz) water, add salt to taste, and bring to the boil. Return the meat rolls to the sauce, cover the pan, and braise over a low heat until tender. Halfway through the cooking time, add the remaining green pepper and tomato.
Lift the meat rolls out of the sauce, place them on a board, and remove the string. Strain the sauce; stir the flour into the soured cream and add this mixture to the sauce, and bring it to the boil. Cut the meat into oblique slices, arrange the slices on a serving dish and cover them with the sauce. Serve immediately, garnished with parsley and slices of green pepper and/or tomato. Serve with dumplings tossed in dill butter or large corn dumplings (see p. 46)
Note: This dish is named after Sándor Csáky, a distinguished 20th century master chef.

TRANSYLVANIAN MEAT PLATTER (Erdélyi fatányéros)

4	fillet steaks
4	veal escalopes
4	pork chops
	salt and pepper
4	thick rashers smoked bacon with rind
100 g (4 oz)	flour
100 ml (4 fl oz)	oil
600 g (1¼lb)	fried potato slices or chips
	a few lettuce leaves
	mixed pickles (gherkins, red and green peppers, etc)
1 tsp	paprika

Wash the meat and wipe it dry, beat it out a little, and sprinkle it with salt and freshly-milled pepper. Score the rind of the bacon, and fry it in a frying pan until the fat melts; keep warm.
Coat the meat slices with the flour. Heat the bacon fat together with the oil, and fry all the meat slices until browned. Heap the fried potatoes in the middle of a large round wooden platter (or 2 small ones), then arrange the meat slices on top. Garnish around the edge of the platter with the lettuce leaves or various different coloured pickles. Dip the fried bacon in the paprika and arrange it on top of the meat.
Serve immediately. The meat can also be grilled, but then don't coat it with flour beforehand.

FILLET STEAKS BUDAPEST STYLE (Budapest bélszín)

1	large onion
2 tbsps	oil
½ tsp	paprika
300 g (11 oz)	chopped veal bones, washed
	salt and pepper
200 g (7 oz)	goose liver
80 g (3 oz)	smoked bacon
200 g (7 oz)	green peppers
200 g (7 oz)	mushrooms
100 g (4 oz)	tomatoes
150 g (5 oz)	peas
800 g (1¾ lb)	fillet of beef
50 g (2 oz)	butter or margarine

For the sauce, chop the onion finely and fry it in the oil until just softened. Sprinkle on the paprika, add the bones, and pour on enough water to cover them. Add a little salt, cover the pan, and simmer over a low heat for 35–40 minutes.
Prepare the ragout: dice the goose liver and the bacon; core and dice the green peppers, wipe and dice the mushrooms, and peel the tomatoes and cut them into thin strips. Fry the bacon, add the green peppers,

mushrooms, tomatoes, peas, and goose liver, and fry over a strong heat for a few minutes. Strain the paprika sauce and pour it over the mixture, add salt and pepper to taste, and simmer for a few minutes, then keep warm.
Remove the membranes from the fillet and cut it into steaks about 3 cm (1 in) thick, then gently flatten them with the palm of your hand. Heat the butter or margarine, and fry the steaks quickly on both sides until they are medium rare (about 5–6 minutes). Arrange the steaks on a warmed serving dish, put 1 tbsp of the ragout on top of each steak and the rest around them, and serve immediately with potato waffles, or chips, or rice mixed with parsley.
Note:
- This is a useful dish when you are expecting guests, as the sauce and the ragout can be prepared in advance, leaving only the frying to be done just before serving.
- You can fry the goose liver separately in a little fat, and cook the peas separately; then add the peas to the goose liver together with a few tbsps of the sauce: this way you can make the dish look more decorative when serving.

BEEF OR PORK PÖRKÖLT (Marha or sertéspörkölt)

800 g (1¾ lb)	leg of beef or pork
2–3 tbsps	oil or fat
2	medium onions (200 g / 7 oz)
1 tsp	paprika
1	tomato
1	green pepper
	salt

Wash and drain the meat, and cut into 2–3 cm (1 in) cubes. Chop the onion and fry it in the fat until softened, then remove the pan from the heat and sprinkle on the paprika. Add the meat, return the pan to the heat, and fry over a strong heat for about 2 minutes, stirring constantly. Then cover the pan, reduce the heat, add salt to taste, and add the tomato and the green pepper (both left whole). The meat should be braised in its own juices – this is what produces the typical pörkölt taste. If the juices should evaporate, replace them with only a little water. By the time the meat is tender, the onion will disintegrate, and the sauce will be thick and almost creamy.
Note: *Pörkölt* is the basis for many Hungarian one-course dishes and soups. Although for these dishes you will generally need less than the quantities given in this recipe, I would strongly recommend that you prepare larger quantities of pörkölt, because the braising time is quite long (200 g / 7 oz of meat takes just as long as 10 times that amount!). Small quantities will keep for months in the freezer, so in the end you will save time and energy by preparing it in bulk.
It's worth knowing that *pörkölt* is a particular type of dish. Essentially it entails frying onions in fat, adding paprika immediately or subsequently, then adding the meat and frying it over a strong heat for a few minutes before braising it in its own juices until tender.
It is often confused with *paprikás*, which is prepared in a slightly different way: once the onions are fried and the paprika is stirred in, a little water is poured on immediately, then salt and seasoning according to the recipe is added, and the mixture is brought to the boil. Only when the liquid boils is the main ingredient – often vegetables rather than meat – added, and it is braised until tender in more liquid than a pörkölt.

RUSTY MEAT WITH CORN DUMPLINGS ("Rozsdás" hús puliszkagaluskával)

800 g (1¾ lb)	rump or fillet steak
4	tbsps oil
4	large onions, peeled and sliced
	salt and pepper
200 ml (7 fl oz)	dry white wine
1–2 tsps	mustard
	For the corn dumplings:
500 ml (1 pint)	water
	salt
150 g (5 oz)	corn meal (polenta)
50 g (2 oz)	butter or margarine
2 tbsps	oil or melted butter
1	small bunch parsley or dill, chopped

Wash the meat and cut it into thin slices or 2 cm (1 in) wide strips. Heat the oil in a saucepan and seal the meat quickly on both sides. Add the onions, salt, and a generous sprinkling of pepper. Stir gently, cover the pan, and braise for 30 minutes. Pour in the wine, and continue braising over a low heat, keeping the pan covered, until the meat is tender, replacing any evaporated liquid with a little water. By the time the meat is tender, the onions will disintegrate to form a tasty, thick sauce. Finally, season with the mustard (be careful – if the wine is very dry, you will need less of the mustard: use just enough to sharpen the sauce slightly), sprinkle on some freshly-milled pepper, return to the boil briefly, and transfer to a warmed deep serving dish.
For the corn dumplings: add 1 tsp salt to the water and bring to the boil. Add the corn meal, stirring constantly, and when it swells and thickens, remove the saucepan from the heat, cover it, and leave it to stand for 5 minutes. Stir in the butter, and then use 2 tbsps dipped in oil to form large dumplings from the mixture. Arrange them on a warmed serving dish, scatter the parsley or dill on top, and serve hot.

Fillet steaks Budapest style

serve mashed potatoes, or dumplings made from semolina cooked in salted milk and mixed with butter; but corn dumplings are best because their sweetish taste brings out the flavour of the food better.

CAULDRON GULYÁS WITH RED WINE (Vörösboros bográcsgulyás)

Serves 6–8

2 kg (4 lb)	beef (tender sirloin, leg, fillet)
100 g (4 oz)	lard or oil
300 g (11 oz)	onions
2 tsps	slightly sharp paprika
200 g (7 oz)	green peppers
200 g (7 oz)	tomatoes
3–4	cloves garlic
1 tsp	caraway seeds
	salt
1	cherry paprika
1 kg (2 lb)	potatoes, peeled and cut into chunks or large cubes
1	pointed (sharp) green pepper

For this dish, what you really need in addition to the ingredients is a cauldron of about 5 litres / 9 pints capacity, and someone to tend the fire underneath it, stoking it up and damping it down as necessary. However, in the absence of these, a large cast iron saucepan and the cooker in the kitchen will do.

Wash and drain the meat, and remove the fat – but not the fine sinews. Cut it into 3 cm (1 in) cubes. Peel the onion, wash and chop it. Warm up the fat a little, and stir the paprika into it. Pour a little fat into the saucepan, then put a layer of meat on top, then a little onion, a few slices of green pepper, some tomato, a little garlic, caraway seeds, and salt; then more paprika/fat mixture, meat, onion, etc. Finally, crumble the cherry paprika over the top. Simmer over a moderate heat – if you are using a saucepan rather than a cauldron, cover it! – but don't stir, just give it a shake occasionally. This requires some patience: the meat will be almost tender after about 1½ hours. At this stage, pour in the wine and add the potatoes, and

Cauldron gulyás with red wine

continue cooking only as long as it takes for the potatoes to soften, by which time they will have absorbed almost all the juices. Serve in the saucepan (or cauldron), garnished with rings of sharp green pepper.

CALF'S LIVER SZAPÁRY STYLE (Borjúmáj Szapáry módra)

8 slices	(about 600 g / 1¼lb) calf's liver
2	pig's kidneys
1	calf's brain
2 tbsps	oil
1	large onion, finely chopped
½ tsp	crumbled marjoram
½ tsp	noble-sweet paprika
1	green pepper, thinly sliced
1	tomato, peeled and cut into strips
	salt and pepper
6–8	tbsps flour
100 ml (4 fl oz)	oil for frying
2–3 sprigs parsley	

Remove the membranes and sinews from the liver. Clean the kidneys, cut them into thin strips, then scald them, rinse them in cold water, and drain them thoroughly. Wash the brain and remove the membranes, then dice it. Fry the onion in the oil until just softened, add the kidney, sprinkle on the marjoram and a little pepper, and fry over a strong heat for about 5 minutes, stirring constantly. Add the paprika, green pepper, tomato, and brain, and continue frying for another 3–4 minutes. Season with salt only at the end; keep warm.
Coat the liver slices with the flour. Heat the oil and fry the liver slices over a moderate heat for 3 minutes on each side. Arrange the slices on a warmed serving dish, and heap equal quantities of the kidney and brain mixture onto each slice.
Garnish with parsley leaves, and serve immediately, accompanied with chips, or mashed potatoes, or rice mixed with parsley. This dish should be eaten as soon as it is ready.
Variations: Use pig's liver or veal fillet steaks instead of the calf's liver.

LUNG SALON STYLE WITH BREAD DUMPLINGS (Szalontüdő zsemlegombóccal)

800 g (1¾ lb)	pig's, calf's, or sheep's lungs
2	large onions, peeled, 1 grated
2	cloves garlic, 1 crushed
	salt and pepper
2	bay leaves
50 g (2 oz)	pickled gherkins, chopped
15–20	capers, chopped
	grated rind and strained juice of ½ lemon
50 g (2 oz)	margarine or oil
5 tbsps	flour
2 tbsps	sugar
½ tsp	paprika
1 tsp	mustard
100 ml (4 fl oz)	soured cream
	For the bread dumplings:
3	dry bread rolls
50 g (2 oz)	butter or margarine or fat
1	small onion
1	small bunch parsley, finely chopped
2	eggs
200 ml (7 fl oz)	milk
	salt and pepper
100 g (4 oz)	flour

Wash the lungs thoroughly, clean them, and put them in a saucepan with enough cold water to cover them. Bring to the boil, then add the whole onion, together with the whole garlic clove and 15–20 peppercorns in an infuser, 1 bay leaf, and salt to taste. Cover the pan, and simmer over a low heat (or in a pressure cooker) until tender. Remove the lungs from the liquid and allow to cool to room temperature.
Meanwhile, heat the fat and brown the flour and sugar in it, stirring constantly. Add the grated onion, the crushed garlic, 1 bay leaf, the gherkins, the capers, and the lemon rind, and fry for a few minutes. Remove from the heat, stir in the paprika, and leave to cool.
Cut the lungs into thin strips. Add 300–400 ml (about ½ pint) of the cooking liquid to the cooled roux and stir until smooth, then reduce over a low heat until thickened to the consistency of a sauce. Sharpen to taste with the mustard and the lemon juice, add the lungs, and simmer for another 10–15 minutes, then check the seasoning and ad sugar if necessary. Place on a warmed serving dish and serve with bread dumplings. Serve the soured cream in a separate bowl.
For the bread dumplings: cut the rolls into 1 cm (½ in) cubes and fry them in half the fat in a large frying pan until golden brown and crisp. Peel and grate the onion and fry it in the remaining fat until just softened, then stir it into the bread cubes together with the parsley. Beat the eggs with the milk, add salt and pepper to taste, and pour the mixture over the bread cubes. Sprinkle on the flour, stir, and leave to stand for 10 minutes. With wet hands form the mixture into round dumplings, using about 1 tbsp of the mixture for each one. Put the dumplings into boiling salted water. When they are done, they will rise to the surface: lift them out with a draining spoon and keep them warm.

PASTA AND PASTRIES

PLUM DUMPLINGS (Szilvás gombóc)

	For 20–25 dumplings
1 kg (2 lb)	potatoes
500 g (1 lb)	plums – use a type which separates easily from the stone
350 g (12 oz)	flour
130 g (4½ oz)	butter or margarine
1 pinch	salt
	flour for rolling out
½ tsp	ground cinnamon
100 g (4 oz)	breadcrumbs
	mixture of caster sugar and cinnamon

Wash the potatoes thoroughly and cook them unpeeled. Meanwhile, wash the plums, dry them with a clean tea towel, and stone them. Drain the potatoes, and peel and mash them while still hot, then leave them to cool to room temperature. Add the flour, 30 g (1 oz) of the butter, and the salt, and knead well. Roll it out on a floured surface to a thickness of 5 mm (¼ inch), and cut it into 6 cm (2½ in) squares. Place a plum in the middle of each square and sprinkle it with a pinch of cinnamon, then lift the corners and pinch them together, and use both hands to roll the pastry-covered plum into a round dumpling. Carefully put half the dumplings into boiling water, and when they rise to the surface, continue cooking for another 3–5 minutes.

Meanwhile, fry the breadcrumbs in the remaining butter until golden, and transfer half of it to a deep bowl. Lift the dumplings out of the water with a draining spoon, drain them thoroughly, put them on top of the breadcrumbs, and cover the bowl. After 2–3 minutes, shake the dish with a loose circular motion, holding the lid on tightly, to coat the dumplings with the breadcrumbs. (During the 2–3 minute resting time, the pastry sets a little, so the dumplings stay dumpling-shaped and don't split so easily.) Cook the second batch of dumplings in the same way, and put these into the pan containing the remaining fried breadcrumbs. Shake the pan after 2–3 minutes to coat the dumplings, and add them to the ones in the serving bowl. Sprinkle with the caster sugar and cinnamon mixture, and serve immediately. This dish is best eaten fresh!

Note:

- If the plums are large, put just half a plum onto each pastry square; if they are a little unripe, put a small sugar cube in the cavity left by the stone.
- For alternative fillings, use apricot quarters, or strawberries, or morello cherries, or grapes; or even thick plum jam.

Plum dumplings

GRENADIER'S PASTA, OR POTATO PASTA (Gránátos kocka or krumplis tészta)

400 g (14 oz)	potatoes
100 g (4 oz)	lard or oil
1	large onion
1 tsp	noble-sweet paprika
	salt and pepper
400 g (14 oz)	pasta squares
2 tbsps	oil

Cook the potatoes unpeeled, then peel them while still hot, leave them to cool, and then grate them coarsely. Chop the onion finely and fry it in the fat or oil until just softened, then remove from the heat, sprinkle on the paprika, and stir in the grated potato. Season with salt and pepper, then heat the mixture thoroughly. Cook the pasta in slightly salted water – add the oil to prevent the pasta sticking together – then drain it and add it to the potato mixture. Stir carefully, and serve hot with pickles or a seasonal salad.

Note: This is one pasta dish which tastes even better if it is browned a little: pour in a little water, cover the pan, and fry over a moderate heat, stirring only occasionally, to allow the bottom to become crisp. Be careful not to heat it too strongly, as it could burn, and then the paprika will give it a bitter taste.

PLUM JAM POCKETS (Szilvalekváros derelye or "barátfüle")

400 g (14 oz)	flour
2	eggs
1 pinch	salt
200 g (7 oz)	plum jam
1	egg white
100 g (4 oz)	butter or margarine
100 g (4 oz)	breadcrumbs
	caster sugar flavoured with cinnamon or vanilla for sprinkling

Combine the flour, salt, and eggs, and knead into a firm, pliable dough, adding a little warm water if necessary. Form a loaf shape, cover it, and leave it to rest for at least 30 minutes.

On a floured surface, roll the dough out into a thin sheet. Fold the sheet in half and then unfold it, and cover one half to prevent it drying out. Spoon small heaps of jam over the other half about 3 cm (1 in) apart, then brush a thin layer of egg white (or water) between the heaps. Fold the other half of the dough back over, and press down firmly between the heaps of filling and at the edges. Use a patterned pastry cutter to cut the dough into squares or triangles. You need to work fairly fast, as the dough will soon dry out and become brittle.

Brown the breadcrumbs in the butter until golden. Cook the pockets for about 10 minutes in plenty of boiling water to which a little salt has been added, then drain them and shake them in the breadcrumbs until well coated. Serve immediately, with caster sugar flavoured with cinnamon or vanilla in a separate bowl.

Filling variations:

- Use 100 g (4 oz) apricot jam mixed with 1 egg yolk to make it less runny. When the pockets are cooked, toss them in 100 g (4 oz) melted butter and then coat them with a mixture of 100 g (4 oz) ground walnuts and 100 g (4 oz) caster sugar.
- Use 250 g (9 oz) curd cheese mixed with 50 g (2 oz) caster sugar, 20 g (1 oz) vanilla sugar, the grated rind of ½ lemon, 1 egg yolk, 20 g (1 oz) raisins soaked in rum and then drained, and 1–2 tbsps breadcrumbs if necessary. Coat the pockets with breadcrumbs browned in butter and sprinkle with flavoured caster sugar.
- Use 150 g (5 oz) ground walnuts or poppy seeds mixed with 100 g (4 oz) caster sugar, raisins, grated lemon rind, and 2 tbsps rum (for the walnut filling) or 2 tbsps lemon juice (for the poppy seed filling). Coat the pockets with breadcrumbs and sprinkle with flavoured caster sugar as above.

COBBLER'S SURPRISE (Vargabéles)

100 g (4 oz)	raisins
400 g (14 oz)	noodles
	salt
80 g (3 oz)	melted butter or margarine
4	eggs, separated
100 g (4 oz)	caster sugar
20 g (1 oz)	vanilla sugar
	grated rind of 1 lemon
500 g (1 lb)	curd cheese, mashed
500 ml (1 pint)	soured cream
8	sheets filo pastry
2–3 tbsps	breadcrumbs
	caster sugar flavoured with vanilla for sprinkling

Soak the raisins in lukewarm water and then drain them. Cook the pasta in plenty of slightly salted water, then drain it, and stir in 2 tbsps butter.

Beat the egg yolks with the caster sugar and vanilla sugar until frothy, then add the lemon rind, curd cheese, soured cream, and raisins. Beat the egg whites with a pinch of salt until stiff, and fold them into the mixture, then gently stir the whole mixture into the pasta.

Grease a medium-sized deep baking tray. Line it with 4 of the filo pastry sheets, folding them to fit the baking tray, and brushing each layer with the melted butter to prevent them sticking. Sprinkle with the breadcrumbs, then spread the pasta mixture on top, and cover with the remaining filo pastry sheets, folded to fit and brushed with melted butter. Brush the top with the last of the butter, and bake in a preheated moderate oven (180°C / 350°F / gas mark 4) for about 30 minutes, until crisp. Leave to stand for 10 minutes, then cut into 10 cm (4 in) squares, sprinkle with the vanilla flavoured caster sugar and serve while still hot.

Note: Instead of filo pastry you could use a short pastry made with 300 g (10 oz) flour, 150 g (5 oz) butter, 80 g (3 oz) caster sugar and 1 egg yolk. Roll it out very thin; fill as above, then brush the top with a beaten egg and prick with a fork.

CURD CHEESE PASTA (Túrós csusza)

400 g (14 oz)	large flat noodles
	(or 400 g (14 oz) flour, salt, and 4 eggs)
100 g (4 oz)	smoked streaky bacon
400 ml (¾ pint)	soured cream
500 g (1 lb)	half fat curd cheese
	salt

If you are making your own pasta, knead the flour with the eggs and a pinch of salt, and roll it out thinly. Leave it to dry for 10–15 minutes, then tear it into pieces about the size of an egg. (If you don't want to

use the pasta immediately, leave the whole sheet to dry until it curls up, then gently break it into pieces and store it in a linen bag.)
Dice the bacon and fry it until the fat melts. Set aside the crackling, and stir half the soured cream into the hot fat. Crumble the curd cheese and salt it lightly.
Cook the pasta in boiling water to which a little salt has been added. When it is done, add it to the fat and soured cream mixture, loosely stir in half the curd cheese, heat it all up, then slide it onto a warmed serving dish. Pour on the remaining soured cream, add the remaining curd cheese and the hot crackling, and serve immediately. This dish is best eaten hot!
Variation: Mix together the cooked pasta, bacon fat, crackling, curd cheese, and soured cream, slide the mixture into a heatproof dish, and spread another 100 ml (4 fl oz) soured cream on top. Cut notches into some thin slices of bacon (leave the rind on so the slices will curl up), and put them on top of the soured cream. Bake in a preheated hot oven (220°C / 425°F / gas mark 6) until the bacon browns. The advantage of this method is that you can prepare the dish in advance and time the baking so that your loved ones are guaranteed piping hot pasta.

CURD CHEESE DUMPLINGS (Túrógombóc)

500 g (1 lb)	curd cheese
4	eggs
1 pinch	salt
150 g (5 oz)	semolina
100 g (4 oz)	butter
100 g (4 oz)	breadcrumbs
200–300 ml	(about ½ pint) soured cream
	caster sugar flavoured with cinnamon or vanilla for sprinkling

Mash the curd cheese, add a pinch of salt, and stir in the eggs one by one, followed by the semolina. Cover, and leave to stand for 1 hour.
Bring some water to the boil in a large saucepan. With wet hands, form egg-sized dumplings from the mixture and place them on a floured tray. Carefully lower some of the dumplings into the boiling water – not too many at a time, as they will swell! – and simmer gently for 15–20 minutes. Test one to see if it is cooked by cutting it in half.
Meanwhile, brown the breadcrumbs in the butter. When the dumplings are cooked, lift them out of the water with a draining spoon, drain them, and place them on a warmed serving dish. Pour on the soured cream, then sprinkle the breadcrumbs and flavoured sugar on top.
The dumplings should be eaten hot, as soon as they are ready. This is a good dish to serve as a second course after a substantial soup.
Note: The raw dumplings freeze well. Place them on a floured tray, put them into the freezer for 1 hour uncovered, then transfer them to labelled freezer bags. Cook them straight from the freezer, you don't need to defrost them first.

CRÊPES GUNDEL STYLE (Gundel palacsinta)

Makes 8–12 crêpes

	For the crêpes:
150 g (5 oz)	flour
3	eggs
1 pinch	salt
300 ml (½ pint)	milk
50 ml (2 fl oz)	rum
2 tbsps	oil
	For the filling:
50 g (2 oz)	raisins
100 ml (4 fl oz)	milk
80 g (3 oz)	sugar
120 g (4 oz)	ground walnuts
1 pinch	ground cinnamon
	grated rind of 1 orange
50 ml (2 fl oz)	rum
	For the sauce:
200 ml (7 fl oz)	double cream
40 g (1 oz)	sugar
3	egg yolks
1 tsp	arrowroot
300 ml (½ pint)	milk
½	vanilla pod
100 g (4 oz)	plain chocolate

Make the crepe mixture by combining the flour, eggs and salt, gradually adding the milk, and stirring until smooth. Cover and leave to stand for 30 minutes.
For the filling, wash the raisins in hot water and drain them. Add the sugar to the milk and bring it to the boil. Add the walnuts, cinnamon, and orange rind, and simmer over a moderate heat for 1 minute. Leave to cool, and then stir in the raisins and the rum.
Stir the rum and the oil into the crepe mixture and make 8–12 crêpes (see p. 16). Spread equal quantities of the filling onto each crepe, then fold them in quarters and arrange them on a heatproof dish. Place them in a moderate oven (180°C / 350°F / gas mark 4) or in the microwave to heat through.
For the sauce, beat the cream until stiff; combine the sugar, egg yolks, arrowroot, and one third of the milk, and beat until frothy. Split the vanilla pod and add it to the rest of the milk, and bring to the boil. Remove the vanilla pod, break the chocolate into pieces and melt it in the hot milk. Add the milk and chocolate to the egg mixture, stirring constantly, and heat only as long as it takes for the sauce to thicken: don't let it boil, or the eggs will separate out. Then remove the pan from the heat and carefully fold in the cream.

Curd cheese pasta

Pour the sauce over the hot pancakes and serve at once.
In restaurants this is usually served as a flambé: a little rum or other alcohol is poured over the top and then lit.
Note:
- In the crepe mixture, some of the milk can be replaced with soda water or sparkling mineral water, this will make the mixture (and the resulting crêpes) thinner.
- This dessert is named after its creator, the Hungarian restaurateur Károly Gundel, the most famous member of a dynasty of restaurateurs.

LAYERED CURD CHEESE CRÊPES
(Rakott túrós palacsinta)

	For the crêpes:
100 g (4 oz)	flour
2	eggs
1 pinch	salt
250 ml (8 fl oz)	milk
1 tbsp	oil
1 tbsp	rum
	For the filling:
50 g (2 oz)	raisins
2 tbsps	rum
3 tbsps	butter or margarine
100 g (4 oz)	sugar
	grated rind of 1 lemon
2	eggs, separated
250 g (9 oz)	curd cheese
	For the sauce:
1	egg
10 g (½ oz)	vanilla sugar
30 g (1 oz)	sugar
100 ml (4 fl oz)	milk
	caster sugar for sprinkling

To make the crepe mixture, combine the flour, eggs, salt, and milk, and stir until smooth. Cover and leave to stand for 15 minutes.
For the filling, wash the raisins in hot water, drain them, wipe them dry, and then sprinkle them with the rum. Grease a fairly shallow heatproof dish with a little of the butter. Beat the remainder with the sugar, lemon rind, and egg yolks until creamy; beat the egg whites until stiff. Mash the curd cheese and add it to the egg cream, together with the raisins and rum, and then carefully fold in the egg whites.
Stir the oil and rum into the crepe mixture, and make 8 crêpes (see p. 16). Divide the filling equally between the crêpes, then roll them up and cut them in half. Lay the crêpes into a heatproof dish, overlapping them a little and keeping the cut ends up.
For the sauce, combine the egg, sugar, vanilla sugar, and milk, and stir until smooth. Pour the sauce over the crêpes and place them in a hot oven (200°C / 400°F / gas mark 6) for 20–25 minutes, until golden. Leave to stand for 5 minutes, then sprinkle with the caster sugar and serve.

STRAWBERRY CRÊPES WITH RUM SAUCE
(Epres palacsinta rumsodóval)
Makes 8 crêpes

	For the crêpes:
100 g (4 oz)	flour
2	eggs
1 pinch	salt
250 ml (8 fl oz)	milk
1 tbsp	oil
1 tbsp	rum
	For the filling:
500 g (1 lb)	strawberries
150 g (5 oz)	sugar
	strained juice of 1 lemon
50 ml (2 fl oz)	white wine
1 tbsp	arrowroot
	For the rum sauce:
3	egg yolks
80 g (3 oz)	sugar
150 ml (¼pint)	rum

To make the crêpes, combine the flour, eggs, salt, and milk, stir until smooth, cover the bowl, and leave the mixture to stand for 15 minutes.
For the filling, wash and drain the strawberries, hull them and cut them into halves or quarters, then place them in a deep bowl. Sprinkle on the caster sugar and the lemon juice, cover, and leave to stand for 30 minutes. Transfer them to a saucepan, and cook them uncovered for 5 minutes. Stir the arrowroot into the wine, pour the mixture onto the strawberries, and return to the boil briefly until thickened. Remove from the heat and keep warm.
Stir the oil and the rum into the crepe mixture, and make 8 crêpes (see p. 16).
For the rum sauce, beat the egg yolks with the sugar until frothy, and add the rum (this will approximately double the volume). Heat the mixture over a pan of simmering water, stirring constantly, until it thickens. Remove it from the heat, and stir it with a whisk for another 5 minutes.
Divide the strawberry cream equally between the pancakes and either fold them in half or roll them up. Place 2 pancakes per person onto separate plates, cover them with the rum sauce, garnish with mint leaves, and serve warm.
Note: Don't overheat the rum sauce, because the eggs will separate out. You can keep it warm in a bowl stood in hot water; or leave it cold and heat the pancakes instead.
Variation: Serve with custard instead of rum sauce.

Strawberry crêpes with rum sauce

MARROW AND POPPY SEED STRUDEL (Tökös-mákos rétes)

Makes 2 small strudels, 12–14 slices

500 g (1 lb)	marrow, shredded
1 tsp	salt
50 g (2 oz)	raisins
100 g (4 oz)	caster sugar
1	level tsp ground cinnamon
100 g (4 oz)	ground poppy seeds
1	lemon
100–120 g	(about 4 oz) butter or margarine
8	sheets filo pastry
4–5 tbsps	breadcrumbs
	caster sugar for sprinkling

Salt the marrow and leave it to stand for 30 minutes; soak the raisins in lukewarm water. Combine the caster sugar and the cinnamon, and add half to the poppy seeds. Wash the lemon thoroughly, grate the rind, and squeeze out and strain the juice. Squeeze out the marrow and add to it the lemon rind, half the lemon juice, and the remaining sugar. Drain and squeeze out the raisins.

Grease a medium-sized baking tray with some of the butter, and melt the remainder. Lay 4 of the filo pastry sheets onto a clean tea towel and brush each sheet lightly with the melted butter. Leaving a 3 cm (1 in) margin around the edges, sprinkle half the breadcrumbs, marrow, raisins, and poppy seeds over the top sheet. Fold in the short edges and then roll up the strudel fairly loosely, using the tea towel.

Carefully lay the strudel into the baking tray and brush with melted butter. Repeat with the remaining filo pastry sheets and filling, then bake in a hot oven (200°C / 400°F / gas mark 6) for 20 minutes until lightly browned.

Leave the strudels in the baking tray to cool to room temperature, then place them on a board, cut them into slices 4–5 cm (2 in) thick, and sprinkle them with caster sugar.

CHERRY STRUDEL (Cseresznyés rétes)

For 2 small strudels, 12–14 slices

00 g (1 lb)	cherries
80 g (3 oz)	walnuts
100 g (4 oz)	caster sugar
½ tsp	ground cinnamon
120 g (6 oz)	butter or margarine
8	sheets ready-made filo pastry
4 tbsps	breadcrumbs
	caster sugar for sprinkling

Wash and drain the cherries, spread them on a tea towel and wipe them dry, then stone them. Chop the walnuts coarsely, and combine the caster sugar with the cinnamon. Lightly grease a medium-sized baking tray with a little of the butter, and melt the rest.
Lay 4 of the filo pastry sheets onto a spotlessly clean tea towel, and use a brush to spot melted butter onto and between the sheets. Sprinkle on 2 tbsps of breadcrumbs, laving a 3 cm (1 in) margin at the edges. Spread half the cherries along one of the long sides of the top sheet (don't cover more than half of the sheet), and sprinkle on half the cinnamon sugar and half the walnuts. Using the tea towel, first fold in the short sides of the pastry sheets, and then roll the strudel lengthwise, not too tightly.
Carefully lay the strudel onto the baking tray and immediately brush it with melted butter. Repeat with the remaining filo pastry sheets and filling, then bake the strudels in a hot oven (200°C / 400°F / gas mark 6) for about 20 minutes, until lightly browned.
Leave the strudels on the baking tray to cool a little, then cut them into 4–5 cm (2 in) slices, sprinkle them with caster sugar, and arrange them on a serving dish. This looks and tastes best when fresh, as the pastry will go soggy if left to stand.

Variation:
- use morello cherries (with more sugar) instead of cherries.

FLAKY SCONES WITH CRACKLING (Leveles tepertős pogácsa)

Makes 40–45

500 g (1 lb)	flour
30 g (1 oz)	fresh yeast
	salt and pepper

Cherry strudel

1	egg
200–300 ml	(about ½ pint) curdled or sour milk, or thin yogurt
300 g (11 oz)	crackling, grated
1	egg for brushing

Sift the flour and crumble the yeast straight into it, then add the egg, 1 tsp salt, and enough sour milk to give a moderately firm dough – you don't need to work it very thoroughly. Form the dough into a loaf shape, cover it with a tea towel and leave it for 30 minutes, then roll it out into a rectangle. Combine the crackling with 1 tsp salt and ½ tsp pepper and spread the mixture over the dough. Next, fold the top third of the dough down over the middle third and the bottom third up on top of it; and then the left third over the middle third and the right third underneath. It doesn't matter which way you fold it, as long as you do it the same way, in the same order, each time – otherwise your pastry won't be flaky. Cover the dough with a tea towel, leave it for 30 minutes, and then repeat the rolling and folding. Do this 4 times in total: the dough will increase in size, and will increasingly form blisters as you roll it. Finally, roll the dough out 3 cm (1 in) thick, cut a criss-cross pattern all over the top with a sharp knife, and cut out rounds with a medium-sized cutter. Place the rounds on a baking sheet a fair distance apart as they will swell (and may even lean) during baking, brush the tops with the egg, and bake in a preheated hot oven (220°C / 425°F / gas mark 7) for 20–25 minutes until nicely browned. They taste best while still warm.

Note: Don't be afraid of all the folding: it's very easy to do, it just takes time – and a batch of delicious scones will do your popularity no end of good!

GOLDEN DUMPLINGS (Aranygaluska)

Serves 6–8

50 g (2 oz)	raisins
250 ml (8 fl oz)	milk
2	sugar cubes
20 g (1 oz)	fresh yeast
300 g (11 oz)	flour
2	eggs
110 g (4 oz)	caster sugar
1 pinch	salt
120 g (4 oz)	butter or margarine
2 tbsps	breadcrumbs
	a little flour
100 g (4 oz)	ground walnuts
	grated rind of 1 lemon
1	egg yolk
	vanilla sugar for sprinkling

Soak the raisins in lukewarm water. Warm the milk, then add the sugar cubes and the yeast to 100 ml (4 fl oz) of the milk and leave to work. Sift the flour and add the yeast and milk. Combine the remaining warm milk, the eggs, 30 g (1 oz) of the caster sugar, the salt, and 30 g (1 oz) of the butter, add this mixture to the flour as well, and knead thoroughly. Cover with a tea towel and leave until doubled in size.

Grease a 2–2.5 litre (4 pint) heatproof dish and sprinkle it with breadcrumbs. Pull and flatten the dough on a floured surface until it is about 1 cm (½ in) thick, and cut out dumplings 5 cm (2 inches) in diameter.

Combine the ground walnuts, the remaining 80 g (3 oz) caster sugar, and the grated lemon rind; drain the raisins; and melt the remaining butter. Dip the dumplings in the butter, roll them in the walnut mixture, and place them side by side in the baking dish. When a layer is completed, scatter raisins over it, then start a new layer of dumplings on top, and so on as long as the ingredients last. Don't sprinkle walnut mixture over the topmost layer, just pour on any remaining melted butter, then cover with a tea towel and leave in a warm place to rise until the dough almost reaches the top of the dish. Then brush with the egg yolk and bake in a preheated moderately hot oven (200°C / 400°F / gas mark 6) for 35–40 minutes, until golden. Leave in the dish to cool to room temperature, then turn onto a serving dish and sprinkle with the vanilla sugar.

You don't need to slice it, just loosen the dumplings a little with a fork and they will fall apart easily. Serve warm or cold, with wine sauce (see p. 63 – use 200 ml / 7 fl oz wine instead of the rum) or thin jam.

WALNUT AND POPPY SEED ROLLS (Diós-mákos kalács)

Makes 2 rolls

300 ml (½ pint)	milk
1	sugar cube
25 g (1 oz)	fresh yeast
500 g (1 lb)	flour
100 ml (4 fl oz)	curdled or sour milk, or thin yogurt
1	egg
1	pinch salt
50 g (2 oz)	caster sugar
100 g (4 oz)	butter or margarine, 80 g (3 oz) of it melted
	flour for rolling out
1	egg yolk for brushing
	For the fillings:
100 g (4 oz)	raisins
300 g (11 oz)	caster sugar
100 ml (4 fl oz)	milk
200 g (7 oz)	ground walnuts
	grated rind and strained juice of 1 lemon
2 tbsps	apricot jam
200 g (7 oz)	ground poppy seeds
2	apples, peeled and coarsely grated

Warm the milk, stir the sugar cube and the yeast into one third of it, and set aside for the yeast to start working. Sift the flour into a deep bowl, make a hollow in the middle, and pour in the yeast mixture. Stir in a little of the surrounding flour, then cover the bowl and leave to stand for 15 minutes. Stir the egg, salt, and caster sugar into the sour milk and add the mixture to the bowl, together with enough of the remaining lukewarm milk to give a moderately soft dough. Knead until the dough begins to form blisters (using the dough hooks on an electric mixer this only takes 5–8 minutes), and then gradually work in the melted butter. Sprinkle a little flour on top of the dough, cover it with a tea towel, and leave it until doubled in size.

Prepare the fillings: soak the raisins in lukewarm water for 30 minutes, and drain thoroughly. Add the caster sugar to the milk and bring it to the boil, then pour half of the mixture into a separate bowl.

For the walnut filling, stir the ground walnuts, the apricot jam, and half of the lemon rind and the raisins into one lot of milk; *for the poppy seed filling,* stir the ground poppy seeds, the lemon juice, and the remaining lemon rind and raisins into the other lot, and then add the apples.

Use the remaining butter or margarine to grease a medium sized deep baking tray. Gently knead the dough on a floured surface, and divide it into two. Roll each half into a rectangle, and spread the walnut filling over one and the poppy seed filling over the other, leaving a margin of 3 cm (1 in) on the long sides. Roll up the dough rectangles, lay them into the baking tray, cover them with a tea towel, and leave them again until they are doubled in size (30–40 minutes). Brush the rolls with the egg yolk, prick them in a few places with a skewer, and bake them in a preheated hot oven (200°C / 400°F / gas mark 6) for about 1 hour. If they start to burn, cover them with foil, but leave them in the oven long enough to bake through. It's not a good idea to open the oven during the first 30 minutes, as the dough will "catch cold" and collapse. Leave the rolls to cool a little in the baking tray, then turn them out onto a rack to cool completely. Slice them fairly thickly.

Walnut and poppy seed rolls

RIGÓ JANCSI

Makes 12–16 pieces

	butter for greasing
6	eggs
120 g (4 oz)	sugar
3 tbsps	cocoa powder
60 g (2 oz)	flour
2 tbsps	caster sugar
100 g (4 oz)	apricot jam
200 g (7 oz)	plain chocolate
2 tbsps	butter
	For the filling:
12 g (½ oz)	gelatine
1 l (1¾ pints)	double cream
8 tbsps	cocoa powder
120 g (4 oz)	caster sugar flavoured with vanilla

Preheat the oven to 180°C / 350°F / gas mark 4. Line a baking tray with greaseproof paper, and grease the paper with the butter. Beat the eggs with the sugar until pale and creamy (this will take 10–12 minutes even with an electric mixer!). Then combine the flour and the cocoa powder, and fold into the egg and sugar mixture carefully, sifting it in a little at a time. Pour the mixture into the baking tray and spread it out evenly to a thickness of 1 cm (½ in), then bake in the oven for 8–10 minutes. Sprinkle the caster sugar over a clean tea towel, turn the sponge onto it and remove the lining paper, then leave to cool.
Heat the apricot jam. Cut the sponge in half, and spread the jam over one half (this will be the top), then leave it to dry. Melt the chocolate in a pan over simmering water, then stir in the butter. Pour it over the half of the sponge which has been "pre-treated" with the jam, spreading it out evenly, and leave until set. Then use a knife which has been dipped in hot water and then dried to cut it into 5 cm (2 in) squares.
Dissolve the gelatine, then add it to the cooled cream, stirring vigorously. Combine the vanilla sugar and cocoa powder, and sift the mixture into the cream, then beat it until stiff. Spread the cream evenly over the other half of the sponge, and leave in a cool place for 30 minutes for the cream to set a little. Then place the chocolate-covered squares in rows on top of the cream, and cut along the squares. Keep it cool until ready to serve.

SOMLÓ SPONGE DUMPLINGS (Somlói galuska)

Serves 10–12

100 g (4 oz)	raisins
100 g (4 oz)	walnuts
500 ml (1 pint)	milk
½	vanilla pod
10 g (½ oz)	gelatine
4	egg yolks
330 g (11 oz)	caster sugar
40 g (2 oz)	flour
200 g (7 oz)	sugar
	grated rind of 1 lemon and 1 orange
200 ml (7 fl oz)	rum
3	ready-made sponge cakes: 1 plain, 1 walnut flavoured, 1 chocolate flavoured
50 g (2 oz)	apricot jam
2 tbsps	cocoa powder
150 g (5 oz)	plain chocolate
400 ml (¾ pint)	double cream, whipped

Soak the raisins in lukewarm water, and chop the walnuts coarsely.
Prepare the vanilla cream: bring the milk to the boil with the split vanilla pod, then cover it and leave to stand for 10 minutes. Meanwhile, dissolve the gelatine. Beat the egg yolks with 80 g (3 oz) of the caster sugar until frothy, then gradually add the flour, strain in the milk, place the bowl over a pan of simmering water, and stir constantly until thickened. Add the gelatine while the cream is still hot, then leave to cool completely.
For the rum sauce, stir the sugar and lemon and orange rind into 250 ml (8 fl oz) water, and bring to the boil. Cool the mixture, and then stir in half of the rum.
Drain the raisins thoroughly. Cut the sponge cakes into sheets of equal size (one of each), about 3 cm (1¼ inch) thick. Pour one third of the rum sauce over the plain sponge, then spread on half the cream and sprinkle on half the raisins and walnuts. Place the chocolate sponge on top, pour on another third of the rum sauce, and add the remaining cream, raisins and walnuts. Finally, cover with the walnut sponge, pour on the remaining rum sauce, spread on the apricot jam, and sprinkle on a thick layer of cocoa powder. Wrap the whole sponge cake loosely in foil, taking care not to damage the top, then refrigerate it overnight.
For the chocolate sauce, break the chocolate into small pieces, add the remaining 250 g (9 oz) caster sugar and 150 ml (¼ pint) water, and bring to the boil over a low heat. Remove from the heat and stir in the remaining rum, then cool the sauce.
Use a tbsp to cut large "dumplings" out of the sponge cake. Heap them up on a plate, pipe rosettes of whipped cream on top and all around, pour on the chocolate sauce, and serve.
Note: This is a bit fiddly, but delicious! It's not worth making in small quantities, as you will have to go through all the stages anyway, so I would recommend it for occasions when you are entertaining a good number of people. It freezes well, preferably before being cut into dumplings, and without the cream and chocolate sauce.

Gerbeaud cake

GERBEAUD CAKE (Gerbeaud-szelet)

Makes about 30 pieces

50 ml (2 fl oz)	milk
1	sugar cube
20 g (1 oz)	fresh yeast
500 g (1 lb)	flour
250 g (8 oz)	margarine
100 g (4 oz)	caster sugar
1	egg
10 g (½ oz)	vanilla sugar
1 pinch	salt
100 ml (4 fl oz)	soured cream
20 g (1 oz)	butter or margarine for greasing
	flour for rolling out
250 g (9 oz)	ground walnuts
200 g (7 oz)	caster sugar
250–300 g	(9–10 oz) apricot jam
200 g (7 oz)	plain chocolate cake covering

Warm the milk, stir in the sugar cube and the yeast, and leave it in a warm place for the yeast to start working. Rub the margarine into the flour, then add the sugar, yeast mixture, egg, vanilla sugar, salt, and soured cream, and knead well. Form 4 loaf shapes, cover them and leave them to rise for 30 minutes.

Grease and flour a baking tray about 25×30 cm (12×16 inches) in size. Combine the ground walnuts and the caster sugar. Roll out one portion of dough and lay it in the baking tray, then spread a third of the apricot jam over it and sprinkle a third of the walnut and sugar mixture on top. Roll out another portion of dough and lay it over the first, then spread another third of the apricot jam over it and sprinkle another third of the walnut and sugar mixture on top. Roll out the next portion of dough and lay it on top of the rest, put the remaining filling on top, and cover with the last portion of dough after you have rolled that out, too. Prick it in a few places with a fork to prevent it blistering, and bake in a preheated moderate oven (180°C / 350°F / gas mark 4) for 35–40 minutes. Leave in the baking tray until completely cooled. Melt the chocolate in a bowl over a pan of simmering water. Spread it evenly on top of the cake, reserving 2 tbsps of it for decorating. When the chocolate on the cake has set, melt the reserved portion again, and use a fork to draw rings with it on top of the cake. Use a knife dipped in hot water to cut square or

rhombus-shaped pieces. This cake keeps very well, and in fact improves over time.
Variation: You could make your own chocolate covering; mix together 150 g (5 oz) sugar, 2 heaped tbsps good quality cocoa powder and 100 ml (4 fl oz) water. Heat the mixture until thickened, leave it to cool a little, then add 150 g (5 oz) butter and 1 tsp oil, stir it until smooth, then spread it over the cake.
Note: This cake is named after its creator, Émile Gerbeaud, who moved from Switzerland to Hungary in the middle of the last century, and married a Hungarian girl. He soon began producing not only fine cakes but also chocolates, and in time he took over the Kugler café and cake shop on Gizella Square (now Vörösmarty tér) in Budapest. Now called Gerbeaud, it is still a popular meeting place and one of Budapest's protected landmarks.

KECSKEMÉT APRICOT DESSERT (Kecskeméti sárgabarack-puding)

For 8

150 ml (¼pint)	bowls
10 g (½ oz)	gelatine
250 ml (8 fl oz)	semi-sweet white wine
7 tbsps	caster sugar
1 pinch	cinnamon
3	cloves
	custard made with 500 ml (1 pint) milk and flavoured with a vanilla pod
1 kg (2 lb)	apricots
3 tbsps	lemon juice
8	almonds, peeled
40 ml (2 fl oz)	apricot brandy (barackpálinka)
1	heaped tsp arrowroot
100–200 ml	(about ¼pint) double cream
10 g (½ oz)	vanilla sugar

Bring 200 ml (7 fl oz) of the wine to the boil with 1 tbsp caster sugar, the cinnamon, and the cloves, then strain it and dissolve half the gelatine in it. Leave it to cool to room temperature, then divide it equally between the bowls, and refrigerate for 30 minutes for the wine to set.
Meanwhile, make up the custard, then dissolve the remaining gelatine and stir it into the custard.
Wash the apricots, scald them for 2 minutes, then peel and stone them, and sprinkle them with the lemon juice. Place an almond in each of 8 apricot halves, in the cavity left by the stone, then place the apricots, cut side down, in the bowls on top of the wine jelly. Chop half of the remaining apricots and pour the brandy over them, then stir them into the custard, and divide the mixture between the bowls. Refrigerate for at least 3 hours.
Process the remaining apricots in a food processor until reduced to a pulp, then add the remaining 2 tbsps caster sugar, and simmer over a low heat for a few minutes. Stir the arrowroot into the remaining wine and add it to the apricot purée. Carry on simmering until the purée thickens, then leave it to cool. To serve, whip the cream with the vanilla sugar until stiff, and put it in a piping bag. Spread 1 or 2 tbsps of the apricot sauce onto each plate, then dip the bowls into hot water and turn the desserts out onto the sauce. Decorate with the whipped cream and mint leaves.

DOBOS GATEAU (Dobos torta)

Makes 16 slices

	For the sponge:
6	eggs, separated
120 g (4 oz)	caster sugar
120 g (4 oz)	flour
30 g (1 oz)	butter, melted and cooled
	butter and flour for the cake tin
	For the cream:
6	eggs
150 g (5 oz)	caster sugar
100 g (4 oz)	grated chocolate (or 200 g / 7 oz caster sugar and 30 g / 1½ oz cocoa powder)
20 g (1 oz)	vanilla sugar
200 g (7 oz)	butter or margarine
	For the glaze:
150 g (5 oz)	sugar
1–2 drops	vinegar
400 ml (¾ pint)	double cream for decorating

To make the sponge, beat the egg yolks with the caster sugar until creamy, then fold in the flour and beaten egg whites alternately, a tbsp at a time, and finally add the melted butter. Grease and flour a loose-bottomed round cake tin and spread a thin layer of the mixture in the bottom. Bake in a preheated moderate oven (180°C / 350°F / gas mark 4) until golden. Use two long-bladed knives or spatulas to slide the sponge off the bottom of the tin, then re-grease and flour it, spread on another thin layer of the sponge mixture and bake it. Repeat until all the mixture is used: you will get about 5–7 thin round sponges. Leave them to cool completely, and set aside the best one for the top layer.
To make the cream, combine the eggs, caster sugar, and chocolate, and stir until smooth. Place the bowl over a pan of simmering water and continue stirring until the mixture thickens, then leave it to cool. Add the butter and the vanilla sugar, and beat until creamy. Spread a layer of cream over each of the sponges except the reserved one, then lay them one on top of the other, and spread the remaining cream around the side of the cake.
To prepare the caramel glaze, melt the sugar with the vinegar until golden, then spread it over the reserved sponge: you need to work fast as the caramel sets

Dobos gateau

quickly. Immediately mark out 16 slices with a hot knife.
When you are ready to serve the cake, beat the cream until stiff, and pipe rosettes around the top of the cake. Use a warmed and buttered knife to cut the marked slices in the caramel-covered sponge, then lay the slices obliquely around the top of the cake, each half-supported by a cream rosette.
Variation: It's quicker if you use the back of a baking tray to make a large sponge sheet (you will need twice as much of the ingredients), and then, using a plate as a template, cut out the rounds while the sponge is still hot. You can then eat the offcuts (e.g. with jam) or use them in other recipes.
Note: If you cover the top layer with chocolate cream instead of the caramel glaze and then sprinkle it with grated chocolate or cake crumbs, your gateau will be Stefánia, not Dobos.
What you should know about this gateau: its creator was the chef, pastrycook, and delicatessen owner József C. Dobos (1847–1924). Although he was also renowned in his lifetime for a bulky – and at the time unique – Hungarian-French cookbook, he was proudest of his gateau – and with good reason!

TOKAJ DELIGHT (Tokaji borhabkrém)

6	egg yolks
100 g (4 oz)	sugar
	juice of 1 lemon
300 ml (½ pint)	white muscat wine
5 g (¼ oz)	gelatine
300 ml (½ pint)	double cream
16	large dessert grapes
12 tbsps	Tokaji Aszú (sweet) wine
1 tsp	grated chocolate

Combine the egg yolks, sugar, lemon juice, and wine, and beat until frothy. Stand the bowl in a pan of boiling water and carry on beating, without stopping for a moment, until the mixture is thick and creamy – take care not to let it boil. Then remove the bowl from the heat, and stir in the gelatine, continuing to stir until it dissolves. Stand the bowl in ice-cold water, and carry on stirring the mixture until it is almost cooled. Whip 200 ml (7 fl oz) of the cream until stiff, and fold it carefully into the mixture.
Wash the grapes and wipe them dry. Set aside 4 for the decoration, then peel the remainder, cut them in half, and remove the pips. Place 3 grapes (6 halves) in each of 4 goblets or champagne glasses, add 2 tbsps of the Tokaji Aszú to each, then pour on the wine cream, smooth the top, and refrigerate for at least 3 hours.
To serve, whip the remaining double cream and put it into a piping bag. Pipe rosettes onto the wine cream, place a grape on top of each, and sprinkle with 2 pinches of grated chocolate.
Variation: This can also be made with other fresh fruit, or candied fruit soaked in a brandy or liqueur whose flavour will complement the dessert, and sprinkled with hundreds and thousands, cocoa powder, chopped almonds, or any other similar delicacy. It's a very elegant dessert: a sure-fire success!

MELON COCKTAIL (Dinnyekoktél)

2.5 kg (5 lb)	watermelon
1 kg (2 lb)	honeydew melon
	caster sugar to taste
	strained juice of 1 lemon
300 ml (½ pint)	aromatic white wine (e.g. muscat)
100 ml (4 fl oz)	apricot brandy (barackpálinka)
10–15	morello cherries (fresh or bottled)
	a few mint leaves

Wash the melons, cut them in half, and remove the pips. Use a melon scoop to form balls from the flesh – remove the pips from the watermelon as far as possible using the tip of a knife – and put them in a deep bowl. Depending on how ripe and sweet the melons are, sprinkle them with caster sugar (or sweetener) if necessary, pour on the lemon juice, the wine, and the brandy, and stir gently. Cover the bowl securely and leave in the refrigerator for 4–6 hours. Just before serving, decorate the top with the morello cherries and washed mint leaves. This is only good when eaten very cold.
Note: Melons must always be carefully wrapped, because they have a penetrating aroma which will otherwise be absorbed by the other foods in the refrigerator.

CONTENTS

FOREWORD 3

SOUPS 5
Tisza fisherman's soup 5
Reveller's fish soup 5
Hungarian style gulyás (goulash) soup 5
Chicken ragout soup with dripped dumplings 6
Újházy chicken soup 6
Sour egg soup 8
Liver dumpling soup 8
Filled pasta pockets for soup 8
Beef soup 9
Potato soup with celery 10
Lebbencs soup 10
Jókai bean soup with csipetke (small dumplings) 12
Mushroom soup with vegetables 13
Palóc soup Gundel style, or Mikszáth soup 13
Soup of pig-trimmings with tarragon 13
Hunter's soup with red wine 14
Cold morello cherry soup 14
Badacsony melon soup 15

STARTERS AND SALADS 15
Hungarian style fried goose liver 15
Mushrooms in breadcrumbs with goose liver 16
Meat-filled pancakes Hortobágy style 16
Stuffed onions Makó style 17
Peppers stuffed with curds 17
Gourmet lettuce salad 18
Cucumber salad with soured cream and garlic 18
Pork in aspic 18

FISH 19
Fried pike-perch crescents 19
Catfish and bacon rolls in garlic and wine sauce 20
Dorozsma miller's carp 20
Trout stuffed with chicken liver 22
Pike in horseradish sauce 22
Balaton pike-perch in creamy mushroom sauce 22

ONE-COURSE MEALS 23
Hungarian style potato bake 23
Paprika potatoes 23
Lecsó 23
Stuffed marrow with dill sauce 23
Stuffed spring kohlrabi 25
Hungarian style stuffed peppers with tomato sauce 26
Stuffed cabbage 26
Székelygulyás 28
Potatoes stuffed with ewe's curds 28
Bácska hash 29

POULTRY AND LAMB 29
Paprika chicken with dumplings 29
Chicken in almond breadcrumbs with potato salad 29
Duck stuffed with cabbage pasta 30
Goose hash with goose drumsticks 30
Stuffed roast goose with braised red cabbage 31
Minced goose liver with apple purée 32
Mutton pörkölt 32

PORK 33
Black pudding and sausage feast with onion mash 33
Óvár pork chops 34
Vine-dresser's pork chops 34
Stuffed loin of pork Csaba style 34
Pork chops with potatoes and lecsó 36
Temesvár pork chops with green beans 36
Pork Bakony style 37
Őrség grill with mushrooms 38
Torda barbecue with cabbage and dill 38
Wheelwright's roast (stuffed pork belly) 38
Pork plait with almonds and quinces 39
Pork Brassó style 39
Pork with prunes in red wine 40
Butcher's stew with tarhonya 40

VEAL AND BEEF 41
Stuffed veal breast 41
Veal Kedvessy style 42
Meat loaf with grapes 42
Stuffed sirloin Szekszárd style 43
Steak Esterházy 43
Cowboy steaks with potato nests 44
Steak with onions 44
Stuffed steak Csáky style 45
Transylvanian meat platter 45
Fillet steaks Budapest style 45
Beef or pork pörkölt 46
Rusty meat with corn dumplings 46
Cauldron gulyás with red wine 48
Calf's liver Szapáry style 49
Lung salon style with bread dumplings 49

PASTA AND PASTRIES 50
Plum dumplings 50
Grenadier's pasta, or potato pasta 50
Plum jam pockets 51
Cobbler's surprise 51
Curd cheese pasta 51
Curd cheese dumplings 52
Crêpes Gundel style 52
Layered curd cheese crêpes 54
Strawberry crêpes with rum sauce 54
Marrow and poppy seed strudel 55
Cherry strudel 56
Flaky scones with crackling 56
Golden dumplings 57
Walnut and poppy seed rolls 57
Rigó Jancsi 59
Somló sponge dumplings 59
Gerbeaud cake 60
Kecskemét apricot dessert 61
Dobos gateau 61
Tokaj delight 63
Melon cocktail 63